AF586924

LEADOSCOPE

Tools for Personal Mastery and Professional Excellence

SONAL SHREE

INDIA • SINGAPORE • MALAYSIA

ISBN
Paperback 979-8-89544-838-0
Hardcase 979-8-89588-251-1

To

My Family

My Eternal Cheerleaders.

Contents

Those steady moves and that watchful eye,
Through trials and tribulations, they may never shy,
They guide with a sense of purpose and grace,
And, as captains, steer the ships to their rightful place.

True leadership starts with leading self,
Be it managing people, health, or wealth,
Integrity and humility must be felt.

With grit and determination, they inspire,
Uplifting those around, to reach higher.
Their conduct and actions act as beacons of light,
Guiding towards things that are just and right.

Real leadership starts with leading self,
And this remains a fact.
Only when we master ourselves,
can we lead others with confidence and tact.

(Author)

Foreword

"Leadership is not about a position, but a person as a whole."

The book *Leadoscope* focuses on exactly this and on how one can work on building their personal leadership traits and harnessing their inner strengths.

The author, Dr. Sonal Shree, has researched deeply and also used her years of experience to delve deeper into the topic of leadership within. She begins by focusing on the "F" word, which is 'failure'. All of us face such moments in our lives, but the failures should always be taken as stepping stones to success.

She has divided the book into chapters or segments that actually take you step by step into identifying your leadership traits and then building on them. I particularly liked the worksheets she has given at the end of every chapter, which help you reflect immediately and jot down your thoughts. The "Action Arsenals" are particularly useful in helping one deal with difficult situations that we face along the journey of becoming leaders and building on our leadership qualities. The "Mindful Musings" at the end of each chapter are like the quick questions you can ask yourself as you finish reading the chapter and reflect on it.

The book is very mindfully written and clearly shows the kind of depth of knowledge the author possesses, and all the experience she has through her teaching role at Symbiosis and as a leadership trainer herself.

Wishing her the very best with this book, which will perhaps become a leadership training manual for institutions to use!

She rightly said... *True leadership starts with leading the self... because leadership is always more about the person than about the role...*

Dr. Kiran Bedi
Indian Police Service officer (Retired)
Former Lieutenant Governor of Puducherry

Preface: Zone-in

The foundation of this book is the 'F' word.

I proposed, my brain disposed!

In May 2022, I completed writing the first manuscript of my book, about 120 pages.

It was time for a little celebration. Those who know me well know I like to celebrate by taking a break from the hustle and bustle of the daily routine at regular intervals.

I wanted to prune the manuscript further one more time. It felt special because I had been working on this special project for months. Balancing a full-time job and writing a book was not easy. Moreover, I did not want to compromise my 7 hours of sleep, so the work got delayed even more. Having a fixed work schedule of 8 hours helped, due to which there was predictability of the exact time I could be at home. I just wanted to write a book.

Not for performance appraisal, but for self-actualisation.

As soon as I finished the first draft, my mind nudged me to take a small break so that I could come back rejuvenated with more creative ideas. Off I went on a 15-day vacation that was over in a jiffy! Have you ever wondered why vacations end so soon, and you yearn for another to recover from the previous one?

I swear it was probably just 2 blinks.

A fortnight later, upon resuming my duties, I thought of further polishing the manuscript.

But, lo and behold, the draft on my PC was nowhere to be found!

C, D, E, F - frantically, I searched all the drives! I even tried scouting for it in my inbox, but to no avail! Multiple keyword searches later, if self-disparagement had a face, I would have personified it right there at that moment.

Yes, my fears were materialising. For the first time in my life, so important a file, something so dear to me, had no backup. Every other useless document stared at my face from those cloud storage systems, but the one that mattered to me the most was gone.

My brain was ageing in the worst possible direction.

Let's give it one more try, thought I, in my desperate search for the missing document for a week, and then more.

The digital excavation of my cluttered desktop and laptop continued in my search for the elusive missing Word document. This exploration evolved into an archaeological dig through layers of misleadingly named files.

Imagine a dimly lit room filled with countless stacks of paper, some neatly organised, others scattered haphazardly across a large wooden table. The air is heavy with the scent of old paper and dust. Among these documents, some are densely packed with text, charts, and graphs, while others are eerily blank, their empty pages serving as a stark contrast. The blank documents are peculiarly labelled with an empty name, adding to the surreal and somewhat disconcerting atmosphere. The overall feeling is one of being lost in an endless sea of paperwork, searching for meaning or perhaps just trying to stay afloat in the overwhelming tide of information.

The only difference is that this scene replays in e-form.

Imagine looking at endless documents, some even blank, yet named '*Very Important*'.

An overall sense pervades of being lost in some endless sea of paperwork, searching out meaning, or maybe just trying to stay afloat in the overwhelming tide of information.

There was "final.docx" nestled between "final1.docx" and "reallyfinal_2.docx", none of which were finally the final ones. Just when I thought I had struck gold with "theabsolutelyfinalone.docx," it turned out to be like a false promise, leading only to its more deceptive sibling, another false one, "thereallyfinalone.docx."

My digital expedition manoeuvred through a swamp of "final" drafts, each more "final" than the last, in a comical parade that tested the limits of my sanity and my poor mouse's scroll wheel.

But. To. No. Avail.

Ah, the joys of modern file management!

I recalled I may have codenamed it something that I had completely forgotten. So much for security concerns! Even a text search did not yield any results.

Was it deleted by mistake?

Perhaps!

Oh wait, I finally spotted it in a USB drive (finalcopy.docx) and clicked on it with double the joy!

How short-lived it was! The file was empty. So was my mind. Blank. There was no backup. I cursed myself umpteenth time. How could I be so careless! To cut a long story short, let me just conclude by saying that, when nothing helped, Phoenix-like, I decided to rise again from the ashes after another week!

Well, not so dramatically!

Did I have any other option?

Yes and no.

One option was to continue cursing and give up.

Another, and the better one: I had a choice to let go, have faith in my abilities, and restart.

'*This could be a new beginning,*' thought I.

I contemplated and wrote a note to myself:

Note to Self: *Increase the number of walnuts and almonds every morning. Do some meditation too because the brain needs to be calmer with more fuel and exercise! Maybe the increased Omega-3s and zen vibes will help unveil the hiding spot of "finalversionIswear.docx.". If not, at least I'll be a healthy person in future to find the missing document amidst zettabytes of digital haystack.*

Now you may be wondering about the relevance of this tale in the book. Remember, I had mentioned the foundation of this book being the F word?

F for Failure in worldly terms.

Such failures hit you in the face, challenging you with these questions:

Is that all you've got? Was this your best shot?

On a more positive note, I consider the present version of the book more special than the lost one. It brings out a fresher perspective and discards any baggage that the previous version may have imbibed. My life is far from over if I stay healthy and alive till the 70s, or possibly beyond. I do not know much about philosophy. My only expertise in it is the deep thinking that comes from within. My observations and reflections transform into a practical thought process, something I like to call *'cool-Phi.'* For me, finding a connection with the so-called nuances of everyday life is therapeutic.

As a congregation of experiences, interactions, observations, dissent, appreciation, setbacks, and joys, this book is to be treated like a mind map of a thought process at various stages during one's personal and professional journey. Spanning years and memories from childhood to the so-called adulthood in figuring things out at self or others' behest, I do hope this ride opens some unrealised, unexplored vistas for you too.

The result of my learnings, reflections, and contemplations is what you have with you. You may marvel at them, have questions, or even disagree. Experiences and perceptions are always subjective and open to agreements, challenges, debates, or further brainstorming.

At the same time, for me, what you feel about it matters!

It would be lovely to hear from you if you could spare some time to share your feedback with me after going through this book. I will be eager to learn more about your thoughts. If my writing strikes a chord with you, please feel free to reach out to me via email sonalysis01@gmail.com, or connect with me on LinkedIn (https://www.linkedin.com/in/sonalshree/)

Acknowledgements

Sometimes I wonder what my life would have been if I were not born on earth. I would have admired this planet with a celestial telescope from heaven's corner office, indulging in getting my wings impeccably dry-cleaned, always ready to soar!

That was not to be.

The higher authorities above the sky had something else in mind for me, involving plans around earthly commutes and early morning prepping for the daily grind.

Never mind new experiences! Let's jump in.

My first bow to the Supreme Power for giving me the golden chance to be on this wonderful planet, to explore it beyond my wildest imagination.

(Traffic jams on Earth? Oh well, this came as a shocker, but then I have made my peace with it!)

Let me start my journey.

The list is long. Fasten your seat belts, and take a deep breath.

My deepest and eternal gratitude goes to my parents for showering me with their unconditional love and providing me with the very best life could offer. Their unwavering support and unshakeable confidence in my abilities have been my greatest source of strength, fuelling me to push forward even in the most challenging times. I owe everything I am today to their tireless efforts, sacrifices, and boundless love. No words can truly capture the depth of my gratitude, but if I could offer one prayer, it would be this: may they always remain by my side as my constant source of love, inspiration, and endless support. Their presence is, and always will be, my greatest blessing. Equally, I am incredibly thankful to my in-laws. Their appreciation, encouragement, and belief in me have given me the strength to spread my wings and fly like a free bird. Their unwavering support system has been a cornerstone in my life, and I can never thank them enough for everything they've done. Their disciplined lifestyle is an inspiration, reminding me of the importance of balance and dedication.

Special thanks to my partner-in-crime (my spouse) for always being there. I am grateful to him for being my true partner in every sense of the word. His confidence in me, patience, and encouragement have been my guiding light, inspiring me to keep pushing forward, even in the face of challenges. Kudos to him for going through the multiple drafts of this book and sharing his candid feedback every single time. It means a lot to me.

A heartfelt thanks to my erudite younger sibling, whose insightful feedback on my manuscript and invaluable brainstorming sessions were integral to this book. His vast knowledge, spanning just about everything, never ceases to amaze me. I am equally thankful to my sister-in-law, whose inputs, steadfast encouragement, and enthusiastic support have further strengthened the positive energy surrounding this project.

My daughter deserves special mention for her immense understanding and patience as I dedicated time to this project. Her presence in my life has always motivated me to be the best version of myself. As promised, she will receive the very first copy of this book, a token of my deep love and gratitude. I am grateful to her for being my greatest motivation and for always believing in me.

As I reach the end of this incredible journey, it is only fitting to express my deep gratitude to my employer for providing me with an environment that fosters growth, creativity, and collaboration. The leadership and unwavering support have been instrumental in shaping my professional journey.

I am deeply appreciative of my amazing colleagues-cum-friends and consider myself incredibly lucky to work alongside such talented, dedicated and downright fun individuals. The shared laughter makes some of the toughest days enjoyable.

Words fail to express how deeply grateful I am to Dr. Kiran Bedi, India's first woman IPS officer (retired) and former Lieutenant Governor of Puducherry, whose remarkable leadership and wisdom have always been a beacon of inspiration. It is truly incredible when leaders of her stature are so simple and gracious. It is an immense honour for me that she graciously agreed to write the foreword for this book (Pinch me!). Her insightful words and unwavering support not only set the perfect tone for the journey within these pages but also captured the very essence of the message I hope to convey. Leaders like her remind us that true greatness lies in humility and the ability to inspire others.

A special shout-out to the incredible team at Notion Press. Their dedication and expertise made this dream a reality!

Last but not the least, my immense gratitude to all my well-wishers and critics, whose influence from childhood to date—both positive and challenging—has shaped my journey and played a significant role in moulding me into who I am today. They have enriched my understanding and strengthened my resilience, helping me navigate both the highs and lows with greater awareness and confidence.

And finally, my dear readers, what can I say? Your time and trust mean the world to me, and I am sincerely indebted to you for giving my first book a chance. The greatest journeys begin with a single step, and I am ever so grateful that you chose to take that step with this book.

Introduction

Welcome to *Leadoscope*, a prismatic journey into developing an understanding of self for personal and professional growth and development. It is an invitation to view leadership through multifaceted lens, much like light streaming through a kaleidoscope! Building the right leadership mindset is akin to the shifting patterns in a medley, fresh and distinct with each turn. Just as the images in a kaleidoscope change with each rotation, your outlook evolves constantly based on the situations you face and the decisions you take. Every challenge or opportunity serves as an opportunity to alter your viewpoint by introducing shades and dimensions to your perspective. Every moment brings its blend of circumstances that require you to stay open minded and adaptable in the face of life's twists and turns. Your way of thinking also transforms over time to bring forth new perspectives and emotions. What makes this journey fascinating is the unpredictability. Every encounter shapes your thoughts and action further and empowers you to navigate life with wisdom and strength. By developing an understanding of just make it self and emotions and by building strength to bounce back from challenges effectively over time, you establish a foundation that continuously grows and adapts to drive you forward confidently.

Leadoscope introduces a holistic approach to leadership that evolves and refines as you progress on your path of mastering self-awareness, empowering you to lead genuinely and create a meaningful influence that endures. This book is a call to embark on a journey towards profound personal leadership by exploring the depths of your character and harnessing your inner strengths.

Why a focus on leading self first?

It comes from personal experience and learning. In the various phases of my life, I too, like many, struggled with the chaos of balancing multiple roles against the frame designed by society that I often compared myself with or got compared with. The more I tried to juggle, the greater became my anger and frustration, even over minor things. *Why was it so difficult to find harmony among the different dimensions of my life? Why did it feel like constantly battling negativity, like the fear of failing or irritation, no matter how hard I tried?*

It wasn't until life threw a significant personal tragedy at me that I began to question the very foundation of my approach to life. This incident forced me to stop and re-evaluate what truly mattered. The things I had taken for granted—health, relationships, inner peace—suddenly took on a new significance. The realisation was that my relentless pursuit of external facets was coming at the cost of my well-being. What I visualised bringing me sanity was being on a quest for learning. Driven by this realisation, learning became my coping mechanism, and gradually, I fell in love with it, almost like a woman possessed. In pursuing a variety of courses, reading countless books, and seeking wisdom from every corner, desperate to find an answer to the inner turmoil that plagued me, I started becoming what I wanted to be. Without even realising it.

Would you like to know the secret I eventually uncovered?

Well, it can seem disappointingly simple to you. Just as Po in *Kung Fu Panda* discovered, there is no secret. The power was within, all along.

Leading, I have understood, is not about controlling others or mastering external circumstances. It is about mastering the self. Without this, life can go haywire. Personal development creates a positive impact on professional development too. The vice versa may or may not be true.

Leading self is about striking a balance between the mind and the heart, between reason and emotion. It's about developing emotional intelligence and resilience which, I believe, act as the remote control of your life and your relationship with the self and others.

Traditional management skills need a boost in today's fast-paced, non-linear path that cannot flourish without a profound understanding of self. An ability to inspire and influence others through authenticity in effort and traits leads to some practical strategies that show a promising commitment to sustainable personal and professional growth.

Ready to deep-dive?

Together, you and I will explore how nature, in its purest form, offers inspiration and lessons in leadership that demand our attention and respect. We will delve into aspects like the importance of communication and storytelling for influence, the art of building and maintaining relationships, the cruciality of seeking help, and also knowing who to seek guidance from.

I understand the dangers of the hedonic treadmill – chasing after fleeting pleasures – and the importance of learning from the past without becoming anchored to it. Moving on is an essential part of personal growth. This journey isn't about finding a magical solution; it's about recognising that the power to lead a fulfilled, balanced life lies within you. It's about working on the delicate equation between your mind and your heart, making peace with the past, and moving forward with clarity and purpose.

Let's discover this path together.

The book has been structured into ten chapters that aim to nudge you towards developing the right leadership disposition. Each chapter provides an immersive exploration of a specific topic followed by an *Actional Arsenal* (toolkit) and *Mindful Musings* (reflective questions). These have been picked for you to reflect on and grow. By clearly segmenting the learning process into comprehensible and actionable parts, my objective is to challenge you to delve deeper into your leadership capabilities and refine them in ways that resonate beyond your immediate environment. The core insights are functional and motivational, aimed at guiding the reader through a structured learning journey while emphasising action and personal accountability to help enhance understanding and engagement about inner leadership. *Chapters 1* and *2* must be understood well before moving on to the others with more practical implications in professional life. The idea is to understand the core before moving on to the auxiliary aspects.

Chapter 1, titled *Beyond Myopia: Power and Balance*, focuses on nature and the power dynamics within it. Embracing power and balance is rooted in one's intrinsic qualities and respect for others. This chapter unpacks how you can harness your originality and align it with your strengths. At the same time, this is to be done by being cognizant of others' strengths and fostering an environment where everyone can thrive. It gives you a sneak peek into life lessons in natural settings.

Chapter 2, titled *The Elemental Forces of Development: Emotions and Letting Go*, is about learning from the past but also moving on to the future. Anyone desirous of developing leadership qualities can learn from these elements and derive lessons in adaptability, flow, passion, balance, and openness. This chapter gives unique insights into how observing the traits associated with these forces and absorbing them can help you gain valuable insights into leadership.

Chapter 3, titled *Managing Mosquito-ism*, is an interesting take on various distractions in personal and professional life and how to navigate them to maintain focus and productivity. This chapter provides insights into cultivating a distraction-free mindset and some practical tools to identify and manage 'mosquitoes.'

Chapter 4, titled *Personal Branding and Pragmatic Humility*, delves into building a strong brand by balancing humility and announcements. It goes beyond the traditional understanding of humility and explores impactful and genuine influence. Authenticity is the pivot around which it revolves. The chapter subtly dissects *how much is too much.*

Chapter 5, titled *Channeling Imposter Syndrome*, addresses the feeling of inadequacy and the undermining of confidence that hinder progress. It elaborates on how to manoeuvre out of this maze by rethinking perceptions and creating possibilities. Tools for embracing your accomplishments and understanding your worth enhance this prospect.

Chapter 6, titled *Communication and Influence*, offers insights into the effectiveness of communication as the cornerstone of influence, fundamental to leadership. Techniques for enhancing these skills, like storytelling and mirroring, have been covered in detail, and a sample communication plan has been included to drive home the idea of clarity and simplicity for building rapport and inspiring others.

Chapter 7, titled *Beyond Boredom: Embracing Possibilities*, busts some myths about boredom. This chapter shows how to harness boredom and do more with it to lead to immense possibilities in life. It has some interesting techniques and perspectives to encourage innovative thoughts and actions. A negative state can be a catalyst for something positive.

Chapter 8, titled *Navigating Relationships*, focuses on how strong relationships are the backbone of successful leadership. This chapter provides insights into building and nurturing relationships, understanding diverse perspectives, and fostering a culture of trust and collaboration.

Chapter 9, titled *Mindset Mastery: Beyond Success and Failure,* explores the role of success and failure as integral to the leadership journey. This chapter encourages you to navigate these experiences, absorb and learn from them, and develop a perspective of turning both opportunities and challenges into alchemists for growth.

Chapter 10, titled *Dilemma and Decision-Making: Filtering the Noise*, is the final chapter of the book. It focuses on the importance of reducing clutter for greater clarity. It highlights the significance of continuous learning, self-improvement and adaptability.

Leadership is not a destination, but an ongoing journey of self-discovery, learning, and evolution. Each chapter of this book provides a piece of the puzzle, offering insights and strategies to help you navigate the complexities of leadership with confidence and grace. By embracing these principles and applying them in your daily life, you will be well-equipped to lead with authenticity, inspire those around you, and achieve lasting success.

The concluding chapter, *The Inner Summit: Mastering Leadership from Within*, can be treated as a concoction. This one is a clean slate without any tools and can be treated as the gist of the book.

The structure of the book is as follows.

Components of Each Chapter	***Description***
Title	*Directly sets the theme for each chapter*
Core Insights	*Explores the main theme suggesting an immersive exploration into the topic and explaining it in detail with examples or anecdotes*
Action Arsenal	*Presents practical, evidence-based tools, emphasizing their essential role in tackling the specific issue mentioned in the chapter.*
Mindful Musings	*Lists self-coaching questions that encourage active engagement and personal application of the chapter's insights.*

I cordially invite you to a unique journey that the book chapters address for developing leadership qualities. Plunge into these to explore practical tools and reflective questions designed to help you internalise and apply the lessons learnt. Whether in a professional space or personal, these pages will challenge you to reflect on your leadership disposition and encourage you to embrace a more holistic approach to personal and professional development.

Leadoscope is a transformative expedition into the heart of what it means to lead, by first learning to lead yourself. I hope that by the end of this book, you will not only gain fresh insights, but also learn how to harmonise these inherent elemental qualities to lead yourself more effectively and authentically. Join me and let us discover together how to harness the incredible power of basic elements to elevate our leadership to new heights. Be prepared to be challenged, inspired, and changed.

Every colour and emerging pattern is worth the view through *Leadoscope* that shows leadership as ever-changing vibrant mosaic of insights, challenges, and growth.

Each shift reveals new possibilities and vibrant patterns of success.

The summit awaits.

I do hope it is worth your time and effort.

Chapter 1

Beyond Myopia: Power and Balance

(Image generated by DALL·E for Leadoscope)

Tim Gallwey, an American tennis coach and the author of The Inner Game of Work, introduced a brilliant equation for performance, which he summed up as follows:

Performance = Potential - Interference

If you wish to understand this formula, observe Nature and how it balances power.

Evolution, biological or societal, has always been about the complex management of power and balance. In the natural world, evolution is measured by the forces of survival and sustenance, and power manifests through the agility quotient. The strong do dominate the weak, but without a balance within ecosystems, there cannot be harmony. Species coexist in varied roles to create the dynamic equilibrium for life to flourish on this planet.

Societal evolution follows a similar pattern. Power structures have always existed, be it in the form of tribal leadership, monarchies, or any other form of governance. Structures have always been important, considering the need to distribute resources equitably to sustain everyone. However, when the scales are not balanced, power becomes too concentrated or imbalanced. To restore the rigged scales, the status quo is challenged to push for the rebalance. Power needs balance to avoid destructive mindsets and forces, while balance, in the absence of power, may result in a lack of dynamism. The right interplay between these elements propels and sustains genuine progress, shaping the world we live in and creating our ecosystems. Distribution of responsibilities and authority equitably helps in avoiding power imbalances to ensure the avoidance of excessive control and domination by a single individual or group and promotes fairness and teamwork. Prioritising long-term benefits over short-term gains cultivates a disposition that aligns with natural principles, fostering an environment where potential can be fully realised. Self-reflection is another necessity here.

Nature has some brilliant lessons in leadership and co-existence. Harmony, sustenance, and interdependence prevail in natural ecosystems. True power and the right outlook lie in adopting a balanced and adaptive approach. Regularly reflecting on your actions and decisions, and eliminating practices that hinder their growth, acts as an enabler of your growth.

The intricate balance of ecosystems has a place for all species. Also, the fact that 99% of the species that ever lived on earth are extinct today highlights the importance of adapting to the changes in environments. A diverse thought process infuses varied perspectives and skills, enhancing problem-solving and innovation. If you understand and respect the balance of power, you can foster a collaborative and productive environment. Assess your strengths and weaknesses, accept your imperfections and setbacks, and use them to find a balance between ambition and compassion, attack and defence, assertion and humility. This balance allows you to navigate both personal challenges and professional interactions with grace and effectiveness. Understanding yourself and others better helps you leverage them strategically to advance mutual goals. Accepting imperfections encourages a realistic self-view and fosters growth. By integrating these elements, you create a dynamic equilibrium in your life that enhances resilience, promotes empathy, and drives success, ultimately fostering a well-rounded and satisfying life experience.

Your evolution will be a pursuit of a meaningful and fulfilling life if you can respect and utilise the strengths of harmony and balance. When setbacks occur, moving on and imbibing them as opportunities for learning will refine your approach.

Nature is self-sustaining, and so is its ecosystem, as a complicated yet systematic web of relationships. All species possess innate potential, akin to the raw energy found in nature. Trees grow tallest when they receive sufficient sunlight and water, free from pollutants. Needless interferences, both internal and external, can significantly hamper performance. In nature, this could be anything from invasive species to harsh weather conditions. Interferences, whether internal like self-doubt and fear, or external like toxic environments and societal pressures, significantly impede performance. For individuals, interference might also come in the form of self-doubt, lack of resources, or negative influences.

The untamed natural landscape teaches us the importance of cultivating positive environments, reducing obstacles, fostering resilience, and promoting continuous growth. Emulating these principles and creating supportive spaces enables individuals to reach their full potential, achieving exceptional performance, just as the bamboos reach for the sky. The migration patterns of birds or fish allow them to adapt to changing weather and other environmental conditions. What can be a better example of team dynamics in which different ants work in different roles with different abilities, whether as workers or soldiers, and adapt to changing conditions?

The diversity of plant species allows bees to gather nectar and be facilitators of pollination to help maintain a healthy network. The biodiversity in the form of plants and animals helps thrive in a rainforest. Similarly, coral reefs form one of the most diverse ecosystems in which thousands of species play a unique role in supporting ocean food webs and sustaining marine life. An additional important lesson is about survival and sustenance, which cannot happen without embracing change and accommodating new perspectives and ideas. There are countless examples through which nature offers valuable leadership lessons right from the importance of diversity and adaptability to creating an overall harmonious balance for all species to prosper. Wolves are known for their cooperative hunting techniques, which require intricate coordination and communication within the pack. A successful hunt relies on each member knowing and performing their role effectively. Within a wolf pack, there is a clear hierarchical structure. The alpha pair leads the pack, making decisions that benefit the entire group, while other members take on specialised roles such as scouts, hunters, and caregivers.

Effective collaboration, communication, and role clarity are key ingredients in their collective success.

Elephants exhibit strong familial bonds and show empathy, often seen in their behaviour of helping injured or young elephants. Elephant herds are typically led by a matriarch, who is often the oldest and most experienced female. She guides the herd, making decisions about when and where to move, especially in search of food and water. Being caring and empathetic helps create a supportive and nurturing environment in which it becomes easier to leverage experience and wisdom and navigate through challenges and uncertainties.

Bees use a democratic process to make decisions, such as choosing a new hive location. Scout bees search for potential sites and communicate their findings through a waggle dance. After this, the entire hive reaches a consensus. Having highly specialised roles is essential for the sustenance and efficiency of the beehive. This highlights the beauty of having diverse skills and strengths to enhance the overall team's performance, contrasting 'diversity' at the team level with 'specialisations' at the individual level as components. Similarly, ant colonies are known as one of the most efficient in operating with remarkable competence. Division of labour and specialised roles help the overall colony. Worker ants look for food, the female worker ants take care of the queen and the young ants, the soldier ants are responsible for protecting the colony, and the queen ant focuses on laying eggs. Ants personify agility and quickly respond to environmental changes and challenges.

Power dynamics in nature are dexterously balanced. Be it jungle or ocean, no single species dominates the entire system. By drawing parallels between the power dynamics and leadership qualities observed in these species and human leadership, we can gain valuable insights. A captivating illustration of this balance is seen in creatures of two different sizes and temperaments: ants and elephants. When elephants consume the leaves of the trees a colony of ants fiercely guides and survives on, in the face of the threat from the former, the latter attacks simply by crawling inside the trunk and other sensitive organs like eyes and ears. This makes elephants vulnerable to bites and irritation, causing significant distress. Conversely, elephants, with their enormous strength, can easily destroy trees where ants reside. This balance of power ensures that neither species gains unchecked dominance, promoting harmony within the ecosystem. The resultant situation serves as a metaphor for a more general reality: dominance or survival is not always determined just by size and power.

In the natural world, strategy, flexibility and occasionally sheer numbers triumph over brute power. The ants use their group might and tactical manoeuvres to protect themselves from much bigger enemies, despite their diminutive size. This is the power of collaboration. It reminds us that strength and size don't necessarily translate into invincibility, both in the natural world and possibly in human endeavour. The tiniest opponents might occasionally prove to be the most difficult. One may conquer the highest peaks and may be considered infallible, and lest we forget, the Davids have proven to be mightier than the Goliaths!

If you are an elephant, you may be powerful but cannot afford to be complacent. Ferociously guard your 'trunk' and weak spots. The ants symbolise the undervalued, the neglected, and the vulnerable. They may even be your mental or physical weaknesses and threats from the most unexpected corners. Don't disregard them. Don't underestimate them. Do not invade their territory, presuming nobody suffers because of you.

Your strengths are unique to you today, but in no time, disruption can take over and hurt you in ways you never expect. Once you learn to recognise others' strengths and value them for what they are, you start learning the importance of collaboration and consideration as sustainable forces. Reliance Jio's entry into the Indian telecom market is a prime example of leveraging collaboration to minimise interferences and maximise potential. The company collaborated with various technology partners, including Samsung for network infrastructure and Qualcomm for chipset development. These collaborations enabled Jio to build a robust and cost-effective network swiftly. Jio also partnered with device manufacturers for affordable smartphones to utilise its services, thus leading to widespread adoption even at the grassroots level. From streaming to news, it has continuously upgraded its value proposition to customers, gaining a massive user base. Jio's success demonstrates how recognising and valuing the strengths of others can lead to sorted and sustained success, much like the symbiotic relationships seen in nature.

Another example is that of Ritesh Agarwal's journey with OYO Rooms, a hotel aggregation-based model that started in 2013 by helping customers book a basic yet hygienic hotel room with good facilities at low fares. Starting OYO at the young age of 19, Agarwal faced numerous challenges, including funding constraints and operational inefficiencies. Understanding his strengths in identifying market gaps and innovating solutions, he also recognised the necessity of leveraging others' expertise. Agarwal was able to identify the areas where growth opportunities could be seized. He was able to make strategic decisions that helped OYO advance. This was seen in his partnering with hotel owners, to whom he provided technological and branding assistance that would improve the standards of their service and, at the same time, boost their occupancy rates. The collaboration standardised an unstandardised sector of budget hotels in India. OYO also worked on developing an efficient booking platform and customer management system through its technology partners to add to the hotel booking experience. Furthermore, Agarwal secured investments from major venture capital firms and strategic partners like SoftBank, which provided not only capital but also valuable guidance and global expansion support. These alliances were crucial in navigating the competitive landscape and scaling operations quickly.

Emulate the cooperative strategies of wolves to enhance teamwork and collaboration within human teams. Take inspiration from the empathy and protective nature of elephant matriarchs to create a supportive and caring leadership style. Adopt the collective decision-making processes of bees to ensure all voices are heard and valued. Learn from the organisational efficiency of ants to streamline operations and improve productivity. Develop the adaptability seen in various species to navigate changing environments and challenges effectively.

The Review Template on the next page is for planning and introspection. It balances multiple approaches for a holistic path to personal development, followed by some more questions for self-reflection. For example, if you wish to develop your leadership skills for team management, you will need to set goals and plan the action steps (e.g., seeking mentorship, reading leadership books, etc.). You may also need to adjust your plans based on what is working and what isn't, with regular assessment of your progress. Use this template to guide your personal and professional growth, drawing inspiration from natural elements like plants, species, and animals, such as elephants for leadership, wisdom, empathy, herd strength, individual strength, calmness, and resilience, or ants for resource management, teamwork, efficiency, work ethics, persistence, and strong networks.

The Review Template

Name: ______________________________ Date: ___________

Place: _____________________

Section 1: Understanding Your Power

What does power mean to you in the context of leading self? (e.g., emotional, intellectual, physical, etc.

____

____

____

____

Step 1: Reflection Questions

a. What areas of your life do you feel most powerful in?

   ____

b. Where do you feel a lack of power or control?

   ____

c. How do you typically use your power – constructively or destructively?

   ____

Step 2: Fill in the table (insert more rows, if needed)

Sr. No.	Areas of Power (where you feel confident and in control)	Reason (why you feel that way and what factors lead to it)	Areas of Powerlessness (where you feel fearful, uncertain, overwhelmed)	Reason (why you feel that way and what factors lead to it)
1				
2				
3				

Step 3: Choose one area from the Areas of Powerlessness column and brainstorm ways to regain power in that area.

____

____

Section 2: Finding Balance in Your Life.

Step 1: Reflection Questions

a. Which areas of your life feel out of balance?

____

b. How does this imbalance impact you?

____

c. What changes can you make to bring more harmony to your life?

____

Step 2: Fill in the following table.

Sr. No.	Areas of Balance (where you feel balanced and in control)	Reason (why you feel that way and what factors lead to it)	Areas of Imbalance (where you feel overwhelmed)	Reason (why you feel that way and what factors lead to it)
1				
2				
3				

Step 3: Develop a plan to address the imbalance, including small, manageable steps.

a. What can help you find that desired balance?

____

b. Who can help?

____

c. How?

____

Section 3: Embracing Evolution

Step 1: Reflection Questions

a. How have you evolved over the past 5 years? What changes have you made?

____

b. What areas of your life do you feel resistant to change? Why?

____

c. What are the potential benefits of embracing change in these areas?

____

Step 2: Action Steps

a. Identify a change you've been avoiding and the reasons behind this avoidance.

b. Create a strategy to approach this change with a positive mindset, breaking it down into smaller steps

The Wheel of Life: Another effective tool is the Wheel of Life, a concept created by Paul J. Meyer, the founder of Success Motivation Institute Inc. This tool gives a visual representation of life mapped on a circle. You can use variations of this to make it relevant to leadership, time management, personal, or professional life. A variation is given as follows.

1. ***Rate each area from a score of 1 to 10 on a scale of 10 (1 - lowest satisfaction and 10 - highest satisfaction/excellent).***

   You may be tempted to justify the scores and reason with your mind. Don't. When you are honest with the scores, you will have taken the first step towards reclaiming your power and balance through self-awareness.

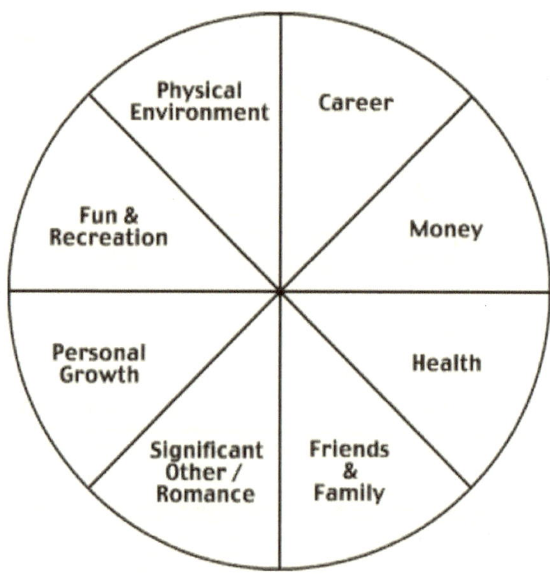

Figure 1: The Wheel of Life

(The photo by PhotoAuthor is licensed under CCYYSA.)

2. ***Write the desired outcomes for your score on each parameter.***
   - Where you are and where you want to be (your score for the current state vs desired state).
   - How can you get to your desired score?
   - What resources can help you? (E.g., Help from coach, mentor, family, friend, learning, certifications)
   - What could be the setbacks, and how to resolve them?
   - Goal setting and commitment to following the steps outlined.

- Person X looks up to me and is in a difficult situation. What will be my advice to X if s/he is feeling lost?
- Imagine observing self from some distance as a third person. What would I say to myself in a particular situation?
- What would my younger self say to my present self?
- What would my older self say to my present self?
- What do I aspire to achieve in my life and how can I start working towards it now?
- Given a chance, who can I nurture? How?
- How can I empower people to lead?
- Which managing style comes naturally to me when faced with difficult situations?
- How can I collaborate for growth and development?
    - With whom?
    - How?

Chapter 2

The Elemental Forces of Development: Emotions and Letting Go

(Image generated by DALL·E for Leadoscope)

Close your eyes and imagine you are walking through thick mud with a burning coal in hand.

Or

Imagine you are alone and extremely hungry. There is food and water, but your hands are tied and you cannot bend.

How do you feel?

These images convey a sense of restriction and extreme frustration, feelings of helplessness or powerlessness.

Would you want to remain in, or break free from, these limiting situations?

Your immediate and automatic reactions to these images are emotions that are interpreted and experienced in the form of feelings (e.g., feeling low after experiencing an emotion like fear or anger).

To cultivate a clear, focused, and purpose-driven disposition, your journey ahead must be into the future without being chained by the past. The obstacles can often come in the form of irritants and triggers. You may experience or relive events leading to regret, shame, guilt, and doubt once again in the present that would keep bothering you and preventing you from moving on.

When you stop measuring yourself against the past, you will start readying yourself for the future. Your past should serve you well, but if it keeps pushing you into the black hole of negativity, you need to push yourself forward by changing your narrative. If you could imagine your renewed avatar, how would you look? With the burden or without it?

Have you ever thought that your present is also a past? Yes, of your future!

Focus on transforming the past of your future, rather than going back again and again to the past that you cannot change.

The human brain, like social media and e-commerce algorithms, too, shows you what you focus on. Try it. Whatever you focus on, be it happiness, sadness, anxiety, or despair, it will deep-dive and extract such memories for you. The stored negative emotions will be heavy and occupy rent-free space in your mind, leaving no space for alternatives. Without addressing the root cause, it will bother you. A crude example here can be using symptomatic solutions like spraying perfume or deodorant to suppress the worst body odour, ultimately creating a far more horrible combo of an entirely new and foul smell that will spell havoc for the nose.

Bringing about simple changes often leads to profound transformation. It may not be easy because as humans, our reptilian brains are still wired to the caves in a survival mode.

Let's go back in time to millions of years ago.

The cavemen and women were always on guard, paying attention to every movement and sound to identify life-threatening situations. Even the rustling of grass or leaves could mean the possible presence of a poisonous snake or a predator and other threats. The emergency response system of the brain was always active because not paying attention could even mean death in jungles. Anything unfamiliar was treated with suspicion and rightfully so because it was all about survival. Today, we no longer need to fight for survival every second (except in unfortunate cases like war zones, or acts of terror). However, our brains still get tilted towards negativity because of the primal instinct that we have not yet conquered fully. Little surprise then why we gravitate more toward sensationalism and negative thoughts than plain vanilla or positive thoughts. This affects one's growth trajectory too because the brain always tethers to the familiar. The results may look like sticking to a sense of certainty and security, living a boxed life, and staying in the comfort zone. At the other end of this spectrum, there would be uncertainty. No prize for guessing what the brain would like to choose even though it may no longer be content with it. This explains why many people hold on to their relationships, jobs or organisations even though they are not happy and satisfied. In extreme manifestation of these cases, they may yearn to break free and scout for something new, exciting and challenging and end up in another rut.

Being mindful of the ways and the sources from which one derives the dopamine rush needs a careful deliberation. Dr. Anna Lembke, in her book *Dopamine Nation: Finding Balance in the Age of Indulgence,* explains this phenomenon beautifully. She mentions about the importance of finding a balance between pain and pleasure in the era of high stimulation available in the form of instant access and gratification, like social media, food, drugs, shopping, smartphones as the "*modern-day hypodermic needle, delivering digital dopamine 24/7 for a wired generation.*"

The idea is not be desperate. Making space for the new takes time, and more if it has quality. Think of the gestation period of dogs and cats versus humans and elephants. The more *matter* you have, the more you will matter in terms of investment of time, energy, and resources.

You cannot see your face clearly in a fogged mirror, just as you cannot focus with distractions.Work on your feelings and emotions to be happy and productive. If you are not in a state to appreciate and utilise the positive resources that your mind and body offer, you will suffer. To be in a resourceful state, ask the following questions for every emotion:

- *Is it worth it?*
- *Is it going to serve me?*
- *Who can I turn to in case I need help?*

To move from the current state to the desired state, you need to make space for the new. Simple changes you make will lead to profound transformation. Emotions, like jealousy, are feedback for you to learn what you like and what you don't. If you feel jealous of someone, and that person makes you feel insecure about something they have that you yearn for but don't have, you can regulate your emotion and channelise it positively by going for self-reflection. The following *Path to Action flowchart* will help you put things into a more balanced and grounded perspective. It can also be used as a decision-making tool.

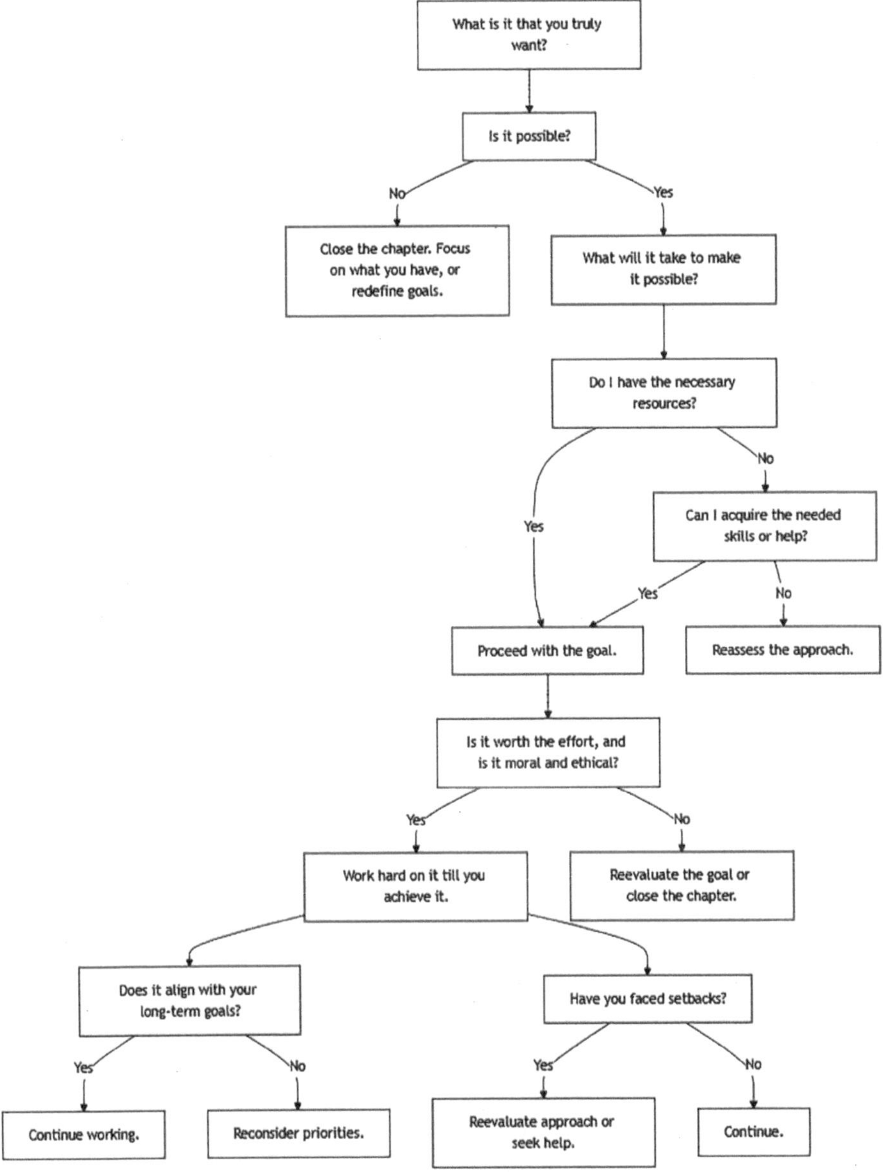

Figure 2: The Path to Action Flowchart

(Author)

In the journey towards the future, as always, there will be supporters and detractors. Treat both as messengers of growth in your life. Their support and the hurdles created on the path will make you stronger. For instance, if some of their actions are causing you annoyance, it is bothersome and distracting. You may choose to ignore it. But if it provokes a strong emotional reaction, which may be related to your deep-seated feelings, it can evoke intense emotions. The latter is a heightened emotional state, rising from underlying and unresolved deeper issues or past experiences. If you've had an extremely unpleasant experience related to public speaking, and you're suddenly asked to address your team, the situation might act as a trigger. It could evoke a strong emotional response, such as panic or fear. In that state, you might act rudely as a defense mechanism to hide your discomfort. Instead, try to face your past and explain your anger instead of just expressing it.

Emotions that lead to self-deprecation are weapons of self-sabotage. In the hands of manipulators, it could be lethal enough to put you in a defensive mode. Remember what happens when the brain perceives any sign of danger? It gets into flight, fight, or freeze mode and will not let you dig deep down to the root cause. Band-aid solutions will not help. In his book, *The Art of Letting Go*, Nick Trenton talks about the technique of watching yourself from the future and looking back at your present self to check if there is any sync between your present actions and future consequences or goals. Letting go of restrictive thoughts, habits, and negative self-scripts is possible when you stop feeding them.

When you learn to label and recognise your emotions (*I am being triggered. I know it will lead to guilt/shame. I need to handle this. I am better than this*), it prepares your brain to get into the logical mode instead of the panic mode associated with perceived threatening situations. You can take steps to handle it with care after that.

Changing your response, taking short breaks, setting boundaries, and explaining can help in handling irritants. Triggers need healing. Grounding techniques, like focusing on your senses, can help for the moment. Professional guidance can gradually help you desensitise yourself to triggers. Professional guidance can help you process past experiences, develop coping strategies, and gradually desensitise yourself to triggers. When you feel overwhelmed, acknowledge it and do not be too hard on yourself. It takes time. The more you open up and appreciate the immense possibilities you have, the better you can heal.

Emotional Mapping with the Wheel: The Wheel of Emotions is based on psychologist Robert Plutchik's model and can be used for developing emotional intelligence (EI), starting with developing an awareness of emotions and then managing and effectively expressing them. The steps are given below:

1. **Understand the Wheel to Identify Emotions:** The centre of the wheel contains the most intense emotions. As you move outward, the emotions become less intense, and the outermost layer often shows combinations of emotions.
   - *Identify: At the end of each day, identify a significant emotion you felt.*
   - *Explore: Use the Wheel to explore its intensity and related emotions.*
   - *Reflect: Write down what caused the emotion and how you responded.*
   - *Plan of Action: Consider how you might respond differently if the emotion arises again*

2. **Regulate your emotions.** If you find yourself stuck in a negative emotion, look at the opposite emotion on the Wheel for guidance on how to shift your mood. For example, if you're feeling fear, look towards the emotions associated with trust to find ways to alleviate your fear. Articulate your feelings more precisely. Instead of saying *'I'm upset,'* you can try to specify, *'I'm frustrated because I feel disrespected.'*

3. **Track your Emotional Patterns:** With practice over a while, you can track your emotional patterns. Are there certain emotions you experience more frequently? The triggers behind those emotions and how they affect your behaviours and decisions? Try practicing with varied scenarios. Consider how you could manage or express your emotions differently next time for a better outcome. Practice using the Wheel in different scenarios. For example, after a challenging interaction at work, take a few minutes to use the Wheel to dissect your emotions and understand what happened.

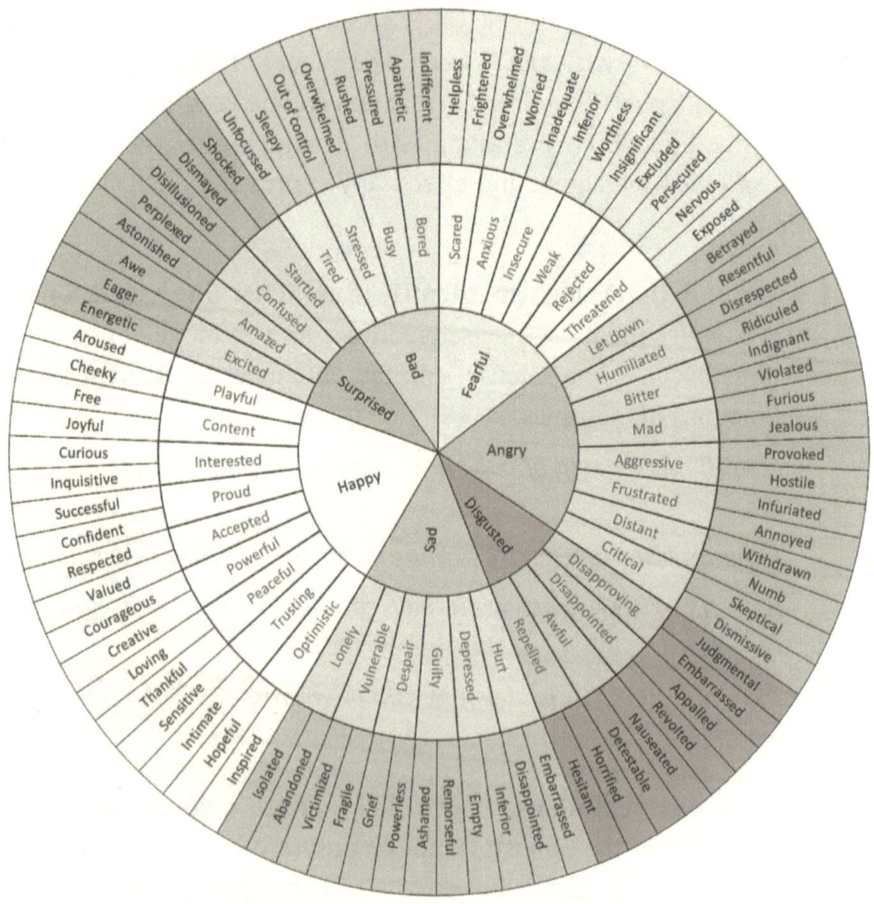

Figure 3: The Wheel of Emotions

Image by @trainingsbyromy on Instagram

Techniques like deep breathing, mindfulness, or reframing your thoughts can help you move from a more intense emotion to a calmer state. Practicing breathing exercises and mindfulness techniques can be beneficial, in managing emotions and restoring inner peace and balance in your life. Their effectiveness lies in their ability to guide you towards a sense of emotional stability through different approaches Each method has its own way of helping you find emotional harmony. When strong emotions such as worry or frustration arise within you and cause tension or a sense of panic in your body, your breathing tends to become quick and shallow as a response to these feelings. Deep breathing exercises can help counteract this by promoting relaxation and slowing down your breath. Take breaths in through your nose and out, through your mouth slowly to activate the part of your system that calms the body down. This action activates a *'rest and digest'* reaction which decreases the levels of stress hormones in the body and fosters a sense of tranquillity. The concept of mindfulness involves being engaged in the moment without any form of criticism or evaluation attached to it. When feelings start to feel consuming thoughts of the past or future arise easily during times. Mindfulness promotes the idea of directing your attention to what's happening in the moment and acknowledging your emotions without letting them take over.

Practicing techniques like focusing on your breathing pattern or paying attention to sensations in your body and the sounds surrounding you can anchor you in the moment. This practice can help interrupt the cycle of heightened emotions and enable you to react with a sense of calmness and composure. Strong emotions are usually triggered by exaggerated thoughts that we have about a situation or event in our lives. Adjusting your viewpoint to see things in a balanced or optimistic way can challenge these automatic thoughts. For example, rather than saying, '*this is a catastrophe*,' you could change the thought to, *'this is challenging but let me find ways to handle it.'* By altering your perspective in this way, you can reduce the intensity of emotions and tackle the situation with clarity and poise.

- ❖ What triggers me? How can I manage it better?
- ❖ What limits am I imposing on myself in my path towards growth and development?
- ❖ What support system can I create to regulate my emotions?
- ❖ In what situations do I feel most emotionally balanced, and how can I create more of those moments?
- ❖ What am I holding onto that no longer serves me or aligns with my current goals?
- ❖ How would my life improve if I chose to release this burden?
- ❖ What small steps can I take today to start the process of letting go?
- ❖ Who/What can help with the above?

Chapter 3

Managing Mosquito-ism

(Image generated by DALL·E for Leadoscope)

Is there anything more irritating than a mosquito relentlessly buzzing around your ears? The relentless nature of a mosquito's buzzing can shatter your peace. God forbid if you run out of repellent, no matter how much effort you put in, it always seems to stay a step ahead of you until you're left tired and doubting your own agility at the end of it all. Trying to shoo away a mosquito feels akin to challenging Roger Federer in a game of tennis—except you're clearly out of the league! The tiny mosquito moves with precision and persistence almost as if it is matching Federer's expert finesse on the court, while you're left swatting at it like an inexperienced player trying to return one of his powerful serves every single time you think you've got it within reach—swoosh! It darts away tauntingly like how Federer hits an unreachable backhand shot.

No matter how much you curse, it will not spare you till you learn how to manage it.

> *In this context, Mosquito-ism may be defined as the habit or tendency to focus on everything, like micromanagement. Be it minor irritants or distractions, it succeeds in preventing you from paying attention to more significant issues and goals.*

It is bothersome when the smallest everyday occurrences sometimes escalate into pandemonium. It can really throw off your game face. You begin your day with optimism but your little world has some other plans. Take for instance that one pen that decides to stop working when you need it most; you end up scribbling until it finally cooperates—only to realize you're out of paper! Let's not forget about the elusive phone charger that mysteriously disappears right as your battery level reaches a mere 1%, turning your search into a thrilling scavenger hunt reminiscent of the final round of an escape room challenge. You know that feeling when your sock decides to play hide and seek inside your shoe just as you're strolling along like a boss? It's like these little annoyances team up against you out of nowhere and suddenly your day is filled with debates with things that can't even talk back!

Your productivity nosedives as you find yourself in a never-ending battle against life's frustrations. Suddenly your laptop insists on an update just before a crucial meeting hits your schedule by storm. Then there's that one note holding project information which decides to play games in the Bermuda Triangle of your desk paper stack (alas, my previous manuscript!).

Don't forget about those notifications that keep popping up for things that could have simply been sent as emails—or even better if they weren't sent at all. The small disruptions may seem blameless initially but they can accumulate over time until you find yourself battling technology, relatives and administrative tasks more often than collaborating with people or doing something more productive. Your productivity takes a hit without warning and instead of motivating your others to excel, you find yourself engaged in a struggle against the annoyances at home and in the workplace.

A formidable but diminutive foe, this mosquito-ism!

There are parallels between organisational settings and life that can easily upset the desired focus and equilibrium. At work, this would be just like the continuous interruptions of unnecessary emails, messages, and meetings that may be just one or tiny, but persistent in distracting you. They disrupt deep thought and productivity, much like the incessant drone of a mosquito. In your personal life, this can take the form of those small, niggling worries that sit in the back of your mind and follow you into the quiet of the night. They are unyielding annoyances, be it in the office or at home, which will test your very patience and concentration. It is easy to get distracted by irritants and letting them overpower you.

True progress lies in your ability to address these issues promptly to maintain your focus on the larger picture. If allowed to overpower, these small problems can escalate and distract. By being vigilant and addressing these minor issues early on, one can prevent them from becoming significant distractions that hinder progress. It's crucial to avoid being blindsided by these seemingly little annoyances.

On another note, some attention to detail ensures that minor irritants are compressed promptly, allowing you to stay focused on the bigger picture. In essence, leading involves not just managing major crises, but recovering from so-called trivial irritants swiftly and decisively. Trying to control everything, or being controlled by everything is a lost game. Delegation and outsourcing help. Leading self involves a great deal of learning how to manage constant irritants in life, ensuring they don't derail your mission. Just as in the case with a mosquito, you sometimes need either to squash the nuisance, or adapt your environment in such a way as to maintain your sanity. The actionable steps mentioned under Action Arsenal will help you take it up step by step.

To effectively manage the "mosquitoes" of workplace and personal life, turning potential distractions into manageable intervals that punctuate productive and focused work sessions is possible through some easy techniques.

I. **Identify Your Mosquitoes:** Whether it's constant social media notifications, unnecessary meetings, or personal habits that lead to procrastination, the objective is to help you identify your distractions that act like mosquitoes, constantly buzzing and disrupting your focus.

Steps:

1. ***List Common Distractions:*** Start by listing common distractions you encounter daily. Examples include:
    - Constant social media notifications,
    - Unnecessary meetings.
    - Email overload.
    - Personal habits, like checking the phone frequently or multitasking,
    - Environmental factors, like noise or clutter,

2. ***Reflection Exercise:***
    - Spend a day tracking your activities and noting when you get distracted. You can use a diary, or a digital journal app like Penzu, or even an Excel sheet regularly to log these moments.
    - Reflect on which distractions occurred most frequently, and how much time was lost.

3. ***Analyse Patterns:*** Identify patterns in the distractions. Are they more frequent at certain times of the day? Do they happen in specific environments or during particular activities?
4. ***Prioritise the Biggest Mosquitoes:*** Prioritise the distractions that have the most significant impact on your productivity. This will help you focus on managing the most disruptive *mosquitoes* first.

II. Mosquito Repellent Strategies: There are some practical strategies as follows to manage these distractions or so-called mosquitoes.

1. ***Set Specific Times for Checking Emails and Social Media:*** This must start by tracking how many times you cannot resist checking your emails and social media. Note how often you check them and how much time you spend on these activities. Understanding your digital habits can help you regulate your time. Designate specific times of the day to check your emails and social media, rather than responding to notifications as they come in. I can afford to turn off my mobile data at 9:30 pm every day. You can choose your time and try to stick to it. The earlier, the better. You can also use *Do Not Disturb* mode on phones and computers to minimise interruptions. Resist the temptation to reply to emails or messages as soon as they arrive, unless in SOS mode. If you can politely communicate your availability and preferred meeting hours to colleagues, stating your commitments, it can relieve you of a lot of headaches.
2. ***Create a Distraction-Free Space:*** Organising your room, wardrobe, or workspace will minimise distractions. This could involve having a clean desk, keeping only necessary items within reach, and removing personal gadgets that aren't work-related. Additionally, you can use productivity tools like Trello to keep tasks organised and in view. Using noise-cancelling headphones can block out environmental noise and create a more focused workspace. Apps like Brain.fm or Noisli can provide background sounds designed to enhance concentration. These apps produce AI generated music to give you instant focus. At the same time, it may not work for everyone. Personally, I need pin-drop silence when I need to concentrate. Any music or background

sound does not help me focus, but many people I know swear by these apps.

3. ***Schedule Breaks:*** Scheduling regular breaks to avoid burnout and maintain focus is a must. Techniques like the Pomodoro Technique, which involves working for 25 minutes and then taking a 5-minute break, can be effective. You can be flexible about what works for you. Consider stepping away from the desk during breaks to recharge. Scheduling breaks trains the mind to focus in short, intense bursts, improving concentration and attention management. Regular breaks help maintain high performance without leading to burnout, which can occur from prolonged periods of stress and irritation. By segmenting the day into dedicated focus periods and breaks, leaders and their teams become more aware of how they use their time, promoting efficiency. Whether it's personal or professional development, reading, or spending quality time with family, uninterrupted blocks of time ensure these activities receive the attention they deserve.

4. ***Eliminate or Manage Unnecessary Meetings:*** Assessing the necessity of meetings before scheduling them should be mandated in every organisation. Whenever it is possible, it is important to ensure meetings are only held when essential and that they are well-organised with a clear agenda. You may not have the authority to control the meeting, but you can engage and ask concise, relevant questions to gain crucial information. Diplomacy and data may help in supporting your suggestions and bringing back the meeting on track if deviating from the main agenda. On a lighter note, if most of the in-person meetings could have been in a plank position, nobody would have had a reason to complain about exceeding the necessary time limit. The idea of having stand-up meetings or shorter meetings with clear agendas to maintain focus and efficiency can help in saving time, energy, and effort.

5. ***Establish Clear Boundaries:*** Setting specific work hours and communicating these to your colleagues and family helps set expectations for your availability and non-availability. Informing in advance is also about being courteous to those who matter. It makes

sense to let people know when you are engaged in deep work and need some time to focus on that. A logical explanation is warranted beforehand if you foresee some disruptions. This also means you need to respect the boundaries set by others. This can encourage a culture where time and productivity are valued by everyone and keep discussions focused and efficient. Being assertive about your need for focus and undisturbed time is crucial, especially when dealing with overbearing people, be it at work or home. Letting people know when their interruptions are manageable and when they are not can help in setting necessary boundaries without any heartburn.

6. ***Health:*** Take care of your physical and mental health. Sometimes, lack of energy and fatigue can lead to irritation, even with a non-irritant element. Your hormones must be balanced for you to be extremely productive and content. For the agility of your body and mind, the desired breaks and relaxation must be non-compromisable.

   An effective technique is to keep at least a bottle filled with 1.5 to 2 litres of water next to you. Having water at regular intervals will ensure that even if you do not wish to get up or take a break, you will have no option but to 'go.' This will be a forced break amidst the unhealthy lifestyle of working while sitting continuously. This applies to everyone, specifically people with sitting jobs. It will be one distraction that your body will thank you for.

7. ***Time Management:*** Building habits that enhance focus, such as starting the day with a clear to-do list, practising mindfulness, or setting specific goals, can help you gain a large control over your day. Moving from one task to the next in the list and clearing each, or grouping similar tasks with dedicated time slots to complete them, helps in organising your day. Hard-hitting situations, tough supervisors, micro-managers, bumpy work conditions, or lumpy surroundings - these are not exactly welcome in life but leave a lot to learn in terms of first-hand lessons. The pain is fleeting, but the rewards are enduring. If handled with stoicism, they offer a plethora of valuable guidance like do-it-yourself (DIY) instructions in life.

Taking a leaf from the Eisenhower matrix, tasks can be managed as follows:

- ***Urgent and Important:*** Handle these first because such tasks need to be your top priority. These have significant consequences if immediate attention is not paid. E.g., deadlines, sudden health issues, handling major client issues, attending to unscheduled yet call for urgent meetings.
- ***Important, but Not Urgent:*** Plan for these tasks through scheduling and strategic thinking as they are important for the long-term but do not require immediate attention. E.g., networking, medical checkups, and training courses.
- ***Urgent, but Not Important:*** Delegate these tasks, if possible, because these tasks, though urgent, are not important for achieving long-term goals. You can manage these by identifying which tasks can be delegated and to whom. E.g., requests that your assistants or support staff can handle, handling some phone calls, and responding to routine inquiries, etc.
- ***Neither Urgent nor Important:*** Consider eliminating, reducing, or deferring such tasks because these tasks are mostly distractions. For example, unproductive meetings, social media scrolling without any purpose, and engaging in unnecessary arguments.

The template to use the Eisenhower matrix for enhanced time management, prioritisation, and task management is as follows. You may print it or download any free editable version available on the web. There are multiple variations available.

Template for Eisenhower matrix

	URGENT	NOT URGENT
	Do	***Schedule***
IMPORTANT	Task 1:	Task 1:
	Task 2:	Task 2:
	Task 3:	Task 3:
	Task 4:	Task 4:
	Task 5:	Task 5:
	Task 6:	Task 6:

	Delegate	***Defer/Delete***
NOT IMPORTANT	Task 1:	Task 1:
	Task 2:	Task 2:
	Task 3:	Task 3:
	Task 4:	Task 4:
	Task 5:	Task 5:
	Task 6:	Task 6:

- What are the three most important tasks I need to accomplish today?
- What are the top irritants that often affect my productivity and what impact do they have on my work?
- How can I break down large tasks into smaller, manageable steps?
- What changes can I make to my environment or schedule to manage these distractions?
- How can I adapt my mindset to effectively manage unavoidable distractions?
- What boundaries need to be established and how can I communicate these effectively to those around me?
- What else can I try to maintain my composure when distractions strike?

Chapter 4

Personal Branding and Pragmatic Humility

(Image generated by DALL·E for Leadoscope)

There is no limit to learning about things, people, surroundings, and the environment. The universe is infinite, and so is knowledge. Your limitation is that you cannot strike a Faustian bargain for infinite knowledge. The more you learn, the more you will discover how much more there is yet to be explored. Much like the joy and happiness derived from spending quality time with your loved ones, deep diving into a continuous journey of learning can bring in a lot of contentment and confidence. The deeper you engage in learning, the more profound and gratifying the returns will be for your growth and development. It will not only enhance personal satisfaction but also foster professional excellence. As you spend more time with people, you also get a chance to learn about the idiosyncrasies that you like and the ones you don't. You may even get confused. Some people may turn out to be the opposite of how you perceived them earlier. This could lead to more questioning because the more you know, the more you realise you don't know. No matter how good you are, you remain just a finite point in the infinity of the universe, a drop in the ocean of knowledge, and there will always be a new learning.

This cements a case for humility. Be humble simply because you don't know it all. Your perceptions will keep tossing and turning as you uncover layer after layer in life. Humility will help you to recognise, appreciate, and analyse the subtle nuances better, as compared to drowning in your own words and actions. When you start exploring the world by doing more, like meeting more people, reading, listening, and observing, your existing beliefs may be challenged. It may also be uncomfortable. You will start understanding and being more inclusive of varied perspectives and move on too at the same time. This will prep you up with an ability to explain things using new lenses. You may even come across ideas that may not have struck earlier. Eureka! Congratulations on striking a gold mine of endless possibilities.

Humility as a soft skill is too subtle for everyone to appreciate it. It directly connects with Self-Awareness, an essential component of Emotional Intelligence. To know yourself better, you need to be desirous of growth and development, and for that, you must be more receptive to improvisation. Is it possible without humility or without acceptance that you cannot be a know-it-all? Being humble makes you an explorer, as you invite others into your world and start expanding your learning horizons without looking down upon them. You treat every interaction and experience as a milestone in a never-ending yet beautiful journey of lifelong learning. More importantly, now you do it minus any bias, because your primary focus is learning from anyone and anywhere. When you make others feel important and give them their due it becomes a key to experiencing a rich kaleidoscope of learning. As you become more open and flexible, you start absorbing deeper knowledge and appreciating varied perspectives. It could well be your exclusive musical space in today's cacophony of self-entitlements.

Humble people, especially leaders, are often better at acknowledging others and their contributions, creating a culture of trust and mutual respect. As they say, actions speak louder than words. They inspire and lead their teams without blowing their trumpet all the time. *Consider the example of a leader who has extensive experience and is meeting a new team that is anxious about a critical project. She has a choice: either to keep talking about what she did in her previous stint, or she may choose to downplay that and emphasise the skills of the team. She can express her confidence and boost the team morale by making members feel valued and confident to share their ideas openly. Here, her humility is calculated and it serves to break the initial barriers to unite the team in its shared purpose, crucial for the project.*

Humility is closely associated with willingness to be adaptable and flexible about learning. It keeps you open to feedback, a key factor in long-term success. This trait helps in building a positive reputation and establishes trust, which contributes to improving interpersonal relationships too. A positive reputation is a great precursor to increased opportunities. The flexible learning curve and openness to improvisation foster a growth mindset that not only helps in gaining self-awareness but also in taking along people and becoming a part of their growth story. *Think of Ratan Tata, an Indian industrialist, philanthropist, and former chairman of Tata Sons.* His image as a genuine, humble, and approachable stalwart has earned him immense respect from the people.

Humility and personal branding may come across as contrasting, yet when effectively combined, they can be incredibly powerful. This partnership can create one of the most authentic personal brands. People, in general, love to connect with those they can identify with. Humility in personal branding leads to presenting oneself with a modest demeanour. Acknowledging strengths, as well as weaknesses, without arrogance or defensiveness, are essential components of self-acceptance and the journey towards learning and development.

Consider the following examples.

- *Leaders who openly share stories of professional setbacks with their greatest learnings or constantly recognise and credit their team for their success.*
- *Leaders who are always learning in a rapidly evolving environment and share their learning journey.*
- *A business owner who regularly seeks feedback from clients and customers, and openly acknowledges areas for improvement.*
- *Thought leaders who actively promote and highlight emerging talents in their industry.*
- *Parents who acknowledge their limitations and encourage their children to explore the world.*
- *Someone who actively connects with the audience on social media and is transparent about failures, and how the subsequent lessons were applied to improvise in future endeavours.*

When you are approachable and encourage others to share their ideas and concerns, it shows openness and highlights the importance of humility. Authenticity and vulnerability are the twin towers this rests on.

There are numerous examples of humble people who have made a name for themselves simply by being true to who they are. They chose to let their authenticity shine through their work. *Take the case of Faisal Khan of Bihar, popularly known as Khan Sir.* He is a popular educator famous for his unique teaching style and accessible content. He regularly posts educational videos of his classes on subjects like history, geopolitics, geography, and current affairs, and needless to say, the engagement translates into millions of subscribers. His sense of humour and relatable everyday examples, especially related to his background and experiences, make learning a sort of infotainment. Providing quality education accessible to millions of students, especially in rural areas, his practical approach to teaching, along with a strong online presence, has helped many students achieve their academic goals. He is a brand in himself without any unnecessary airs about him.

Another popular influencer, who calls himself a de-influencer, is *Revant Himatsingka*, who quit his million-dollar job in the USA to return to India to debunk food myths and false claims made by brands. He is promoting healthy eating habits and encouraging people to read labels behind the food packaging. He shares informative posts about nutrition, wellness tips, and healthy lifestyle hacks. Revant focuses on creating content that educates his audience about healthy eating habits and the science behind nutrition. He breaks down intricate nutritional information into simple, digestible pieces. His reels often include debunking popular food myths and misconceptions and providing evidence-based information to his followers.

What is common between these two people is their ability to break down complex topics into simpler and relatable bits for others. This is a talent that must be mastered by all knowledgeable individuals.

There are several other examples. Known as the *mother for orphans*, *Sindhutai Sapkal* was raised in poverty and experienced homelessness following her abandonment by her husband. However, she transformed her challenges into opportunities by committing herself to caring for more than 1500 orphaned children and ensuring they had shelter and access to education. Sapkal lived a life filled with humility and compassion till she passed away in January 2022. *Chhavi Rajawat*, an MBA, chose to leave her job and become the Sarpanch (elected head of a village) of a place called Soda in Rajasthan at the age of 30. She has dedicated herself to enhancing education, waste management and infrastructure in her village opting to help her community. Despite accomplishing much, she remains closely connected to her roots in the village and continues to contribute to rural development endeavours. *Phoolbasan Bai Yadav*, a Padma Shri awardee, a social worker and founder of an NGO, Maa Bamleshwari Janhit Kare Samiti, rose from humble beginnings to become a community leader in Chhattisgarh by establishing self-help groups that support rural women with various opportunities such as livelihood initiatives and access to healthcare and education services. Despite her impact on so many lives and her remarkable leadership skills, she continues to show humility and unwavering commitment to her roots, in the local community.

These men and women have accomplished feats by showing determination and resilience while staying connected to people. They exemplify how genuine leadership can stem from modesty and a strong drive to create an impact. Boasting kills this spirit. A branding that does not need flashy displays is a quiet yet powerful testament to your expertise and dedication to helping others understand and appreciate your magnetism. It highlights how humility can become the very foundation of personal branding. When you can build a strong personal brand that is rooted in unpretentiousness, it builds better credibility. Humility can enhance your appeal as it makes you more relatable, positioning you both as successful yet grounded. It's crucial to find a ground where you can showcase your skills without being arrogant or self-centered. Being humble doesn't involve fading into the shadows or concealing your achievements; it is about presenting them in a manner that exudes confidence without being boastful. You can embody humility while also highlighting your skills by demonstrating your expertise through your actions and effective communication. It's not about promoting oneself but more about enabling others to recognize the significance of your contributions and inspiring them. When you speak up at moments and share your thoughts clearly and confidently, you make sure that your input is valued and recognised without losing sight of your modesty.

In today's era of social media, if people do not learn about you, they will not be able to have much idea about the levels of your self-assurance. Projecting confidence in a way that people can learn from inspires trust and respect. Being excessively humble may not work in cases where others undermine your competence and authority. Striking the right balance is crucial. Extreme modesty might lead others to undervalue your contributions or expertise. The essential solution here is pragmatic humility. *Sudha Murthy, a renowned Indian author, philanthropist, and former chairperson of the Infosys Foundation*, is known for her modesty and humility, often downplaying her contributions. However, she highlights her efforts in philanthropy and education by sharing stories from her life. This inspires and helps others understand and acknowledge her work. You can showcase your achievements in a manner that feels authentic and modest, yet still conveys strength and reliability.

Effectively communicating your vision and letting them know about your progress and achievements is also needed to prevent being overshadowed by more assertive team members or colleagues. Humility isn't in self-deprecation or in showing a lack of competence when you are praised. People may start taking you for granted, and your superiors may even stop giving credit to you in public. This can come in the way of your growth due to the negative perception it may create about you, especially in cultures that reward extroverts-cum-high achievers more versus introverts-cum-high achievers. It is important to be vocal about your ideas and accomplishments and be able to present them as your advocate because nobody else will do it for you. This is to ensure that your contributions are valued, and people do not take you for granted.

Compare these two declarations on social media.

Option 1: I am deeply humbled to receive the award, XYZ.

Nothing proclaims humility like a public declaration of how humbled you are to receive an award, right? 😉

Try something like this the next time, without using the word humility in any form.

Option 2: I am incredibly grateful for this award, XYZ. It's an honour to be recognised, and I want to thank everyone who supported and believed in me... <followed by story>

This approach not only attracts respect and admiration but builds credibility, which is a key component of a strong personal brand. In summary, while humility is a valuable trait that fosters cooperation and respect, it is important to balance it with self-confidence and assertiveness. This balance enables you to maintain your authority, ensure your competence is recognised, and effectively contribute to your professional and personal endeavours.

(Image generated by DALL·E for Leadoscope)

Humans do not have magic in their veins to help them decode your qualities and achievements automatically. Telepathy too does not work here. People may not have all the time and energy or inclination to learn about your strengths in the organisation or society. You have to take the onus to let them know. Nobody else will do it for you if you don't. In a competitive world, you need to ensure that your contributions, skills, and accomplishments do not go unnoticed. The humble ones may not feel right about it because self-promotion to them will seem difficult. However, the good news is that it can be done in ways you can live with. Maintaining this balance in life is much like tuning the strings of a musical instrument. If you tighten the strings too much, they may snap under pressure; if you leave them too loose, they won't produce the right sound. The same goes for your approach to personal branding. Push yourself too hard, and you risk burnout, hold back too much, and people may never bother to appreciate your full potential. It's about finding that sweet spot—where there's enough tension to drive focus and ambition, but enough flexibility to allow for creativity, rest, and growth. Just like the guitar, life plays its best melodies when balanced perfectly. The Action Arsenal will show you the *how* of it if you are not comfortable with branding yourself.

When you present your achievements with facts, you own your uniqueness. The way you present yourself needn't be an exercise in cacophony. Here are some of the ways to do self-promotion and self-branding for you even if you do not feel comfortable with these initially.

1. ***Internalise the Truth about Branding:*** It may be an injustice if you are not telling people about your skills and capabilities they can benefit from. Consider this. If you have a remedy for something and yet, out of hesitancy, you do not let others know about this, it is unfair. There may have been others who could have learnt from you. Consider it a way of contributing rather than inflating your ego. When people know they can rely on you for something, it is one of the greatest supports you can provide to them.
2. ***Use Your Narrative Superpower:*** You can be genuine when you share your stories that strike a chord with people. Share stories about your journey, the setbacks, and how you overcame challenges to reach where you are today. You don't have to scale a mountain or reach heights to make a difference. The struggles you face every day and the victories you achieve, the setbacks you encounter- all carry lessons that resonate with others and offer opportunities for learning. Sometimes it is in the seemingly everyday moments where we find extraordinary wisdom. By opening up about your experiences and sharing your story with others you encourage them to reflect upon their own paths and grow from what you have gone through. When people can relate to you, they begin trusting you more. You can be

real and relatable when you give credit for your success and learnings to teams and other people in your life.

3. ***Ask for Testimonials**:* This can be done easily with those who have seen your growth and know you well. Treat testimonials as your spokesperson who would do the talking for you on social media profiles like LinkedIn. Similarly, you can have your own blog or website for regularly updating it with your learnings. This will help the visitors. When they come across your profile, learning about your skills and achievements will give them a fair idea of what to expect from you. Do not shy away from highlighting endorsements because they can be as powerful as your digital print. The best part - *you do not have to say a thing here!* The testimonials will do all the talking.
4. ***Use the Word Help**:* Use a pinpointed approach when you write or talk about your impact on people or projects. For instance, *I have helped over 5000 entrepreneurs scale up their businesses profitably by <add a number>, or I help leaders conquer Imposter Syndrome, or I help businesses grow their online presence by <add a number>, or I help enhance team productivity through data-driven insights.* Using *help* creates a positive tone and focuses on support, collaboration, and impact. A slightly different approach I had once used on my LinkedIn bio was 'Helping no one.' This made people curious. The implication was to my role as a coach who does not tell a coachee what to do but asks the right questions. The coachee, in ruminating over those questions, comes up with the micro moments of truth that often contain solutions. In that sense, it is the coachee who helped himself/herself. However, as an afterthought to avoid people perceiving it negatively and thinking I didn't want to help anyone, I revised my bio.
5. ***Become a Thought Leader***: Share your knowledge and insights with everyone, both online and offline. Talk and write about things you are passionate about. Create informational content. Be of value so that people turn to you for your expertise. Leverage social media to the fullest. The then Prime Minister of New Zealand, Jacinda Ardern, used Facebook Live to communicate with citizens during

the COVID-19 pandemic, which was widely hailed by everyone. People respect you when they know you come down from the ivory tower to be with them. They start listening to you. When you mentor and support others, you can play a vital role in developing a culture of learning and uplifting. Propose new ideas and lead initiatives by offering solutions to challenges faced by others. Develop awareness by reading, listening, and having insightful discussions with people.

6. ***Write:*** When you find talking about your achievements awkward, write about it. In organisations, you can identify the right recipients and write an email to them to highlight your contribution or share your observations and ideas to improve something (a process, product, or service). Doing so in writing also creates evidence that can be used, if needed, as a record of your communication. Who knows, it may even help with your next promotion! Social Media is a powerful tool to share. When you post about something you have learnt, or others may have learnt from you, it helps you in developing confidence to lead others, and eventually your own life and business. When you start weaving your narratives carefully, it builds bridges and connections. You may not get thousands of followers initially, but organic growth too will make people sit up and notice sooner or later. It all begins with that courage to hit the post button.

An important aspect to keep in mind is that in the realm of pragmatic humility, sharing one's knowledge and achievements with others these days is not essentially boasting. It may work more as a tool to inspire and empower those around you. When you strike a balance between confidence and modesty with the right intent to uplift rather than to only to self-promote, you can do it effectively. Focus on bringing out the lessons learnt and the challenges overcome, rather than just the successes themselves. Make it relatable. People are interested in the journey rather than only the outcome. You can talk about your mistakes and failures. Adding a measured dose of vulnerability to the extent of your comfort can often build more connections. The idea is to provide value in the form of guidance, igniting motivation, or simply showing that anyone can succeed. The most genuine humility is in sharing. It should reflect in your willingness to help others grow. When you can acknowledge the role of others in making your journey successful, think of this story: *The Unyielding Bottle Cap.*

In a kitchen scene stood a cluster of individuals huddled around a stubborn bottle with a tightly sealed cap on top of it. One by one they took turns trying to twist it. The father tried first with a determined grip that yielded no results; then the mother followed suit with all her might but to no avail. Even the older sibling attempted various methods but couldn't manage to open it either. The youngest child observed all the attempts and then requested a turn herself after being inspired by others' efforts. She used her hands and a look of determination as she twisted the cap when it opened effortlessly to everyone's amazement.

The child beamed with excitement and pride on her face while her father smiled knowingly and commented: 'You did a fantastic job!'

The elder sibling said- 'we all helped you loosen the cap.'

Everyone smiled.

The child stopped for a moment and understood the reality behind her brother's words. It wasn't solely her effort that uncorked the bottle but rather the combined determination of those who had attempted before her that ultimately enabled the final turn to succeed.

Life is a journey where success is often a result of our hard work intertwined with the support and influence of those around us who guide or challenge us along the way. They all contribute significantly to our personal growth and development. Acknowledging and valuing the impact others have on our path is essential for understanding and cherishing the entire experience and inspiring others on the way. You can choose to use your efforts, stories, and achievements as a beacon to light their path, not just as a spotlight on your own.

- Am I respected because of my formal position? If, tomorrow, I do not have this position, will people rally behind me?
- How can I make learning a natural and enjoyable part of my routine?
- In what ways can I cultivate a love for constantly learning something new from every source and everyone?
- How has my image evolved over the years and what factors have influenced these changes?
- What is my primary focus? What stories or experiences can I share that illustrate my key messages and values to showcase my personality?
- How do I react when someone criticises or challenges my ideas?
- How can I reach out to seek help from someone who can guide me?

Chapter 5

Channeling Imposter Syndrome

(Image generated by DALL·E for Leadoscope)

You have always been the best.

And yet, it may happen in life at some point that you may feel nothing makes sense. The feeling of inadequacy, which is not a true reflection of your abilities, sets in. A distorted version of self is created by comparison, self-perception and perfection.

Consider the following example.

> *Let's say you are a bright student from a small town from a middle-class background and have done well academically. You get admission to study in a top university in a metropolitan city. Despite excelling academically earlier, your lack of fluency in English and the pace of the urban lifestyle make you feel out of place. On top of that, your peers seem extremely confident, and you start doubting your worth. Everything seems hazy to you, and you feel lost in the maze. At worst, it becomes increasingly difficult to uphold faith and confidence in yourself. Your self-esteem and sense of self-worth reach their nadir, and you start wondering if you are meant for the life that you are leading. You start wondering if it is all worth it. In extreme situations, it can manifest itself in the form of escapism or depression, and that unsettling sense of 'I don't know enough,' and 'I'm just pretending.'*

So many people face it - the looming fear that everyone will eventually see the real you or the hesitation to step up for new opportunities. Imposter syndrome can feel like a cunning illusion. It is that voice of self-doubt that often overshadows your greatest achievements. It thrives on the fear that you are undeserving of your success, so much so that you begin questioning your worth, despite evidence to the contrary. Feeling like an imposter is akin to being thrust into the spotlight of a play without trying out for the lead role and constantly anticipating being called out and removed from the stage in every scene you're in. As a woman, for instance, managing both a job and a home life successfully can be challenging at times even when you ace that work presentation.

Being part of some WhatsApp groups can often feel like participating in a high-speed relay race without anyone passing you the baton. Let's say, you are a member of a WhatsApp group of the moms of students in your child's school. Some mothers may appear to have so much awareness of every little detail, like recent circulars and assignment deadlines, and you feel lost thinking- *which deadline or circular were they talking about?* You may find yourself going through loads of messages from weeks ago and wondering how you missed this agenda and how everyone else remembered it. When a notification shows up for a deadline that you have no clue about, it's like being a mom suddenly facing challenges and trying to catch up, while others are already planning the event. It's moments like these where you question even your basic qualifications to be the CEO of your life, or a mother. Despite being a pro at multitasking for years, there's always that doubt that a little mistake or missed deadline might expose you as an imposter trying to navigate it all.

Steering life often feels like a balancing act of projecting confidence in moments of uncertainty and self-doubt. It's as if there is a feeling that at any moment someone might question your presence and abilities in situations. Be it at work or in the comfort of your own home, amidst the chaos of daily routines and unexpected moments of joy, that persistent imposter syndrome keeps whispering doubts in your ear asking, *are you sure this isn't luck? Are you doing enough? Are you being 'good?'* You catch yourself excessively preparing for every situation, be it a high stakes presentation in the boardroom, or ensuring your house, or image, are picture perfect because you fear someone might uncover your facade. Not to forget those moments in meetings when you confidently respond to a query only to later doubt yourself akin to making a guess on a game show. Sometimes it seems like everyone views you as a powerhouse of energy and determination, yet down inside, you can't! You may even question yourself at times *is this truly who I am meant to be?*

As you navigate this internal battle, you realise, with the help of support from your well-wishers, that you need to first calm down and stop doubting and feeling guilty about everything. Later, you can focus on aspects where you need to work harder and challenge the narrative that diminishes your achievements. This is how you start working on yourself and celebrating your journey of learning. Thriving in any environment comes with confidence and celebration of your unique abilities. This is life - it's beautiful, yet fraught with challenges. Life's difficulties exist precisely because you wake up each day and breathe. In the silence that follows when the heart monitor flatlines, all troubles dissolve. While living beings navigate a constant stream of problems and uncertainties, those who are dead rest, free from such burdens. It is in the act of living that we face and overcome life's obstacles. Hope makes life worth living, and problems worth solving!

We cannot avoid pricks, but we can surely learn how to manage them. Not all pricks are harmful. Consider how some of life's greatest lessons are like vaccination. The initial jab may sting and bring tears, but the transient discomfort pales in comparison to the lasting benefits. Doubts are those punctures from which one cannot escape. Like the two sides of a coin, they can bring out both the best and the worst in human beings. Life lessons may hurt now, yet they fortify us into becoming a much stronger version of ourselves against future challenges. Ultimately, it is about choices.

Your choices among the 3 Fs of survival: fight, flight, or freeze – or, to face, and even walk away gracefully – will determine the consequences. The tools with which you equip yourself, and the support system that you create around you, will determine your sanity, happiness, and success in this journey. Who you turn to for advice will also determine your mental wellness and growth trajectory in life. We often overestimate our capacity to handle everything with ease. It doesn't hurt to ask for help. Even the most successful people and organisations need to open their ears and minds to varied perspectives. It is important to be able to separate the wheat from the chaff.

Leaders are often surrounded by their in-group, who may largely influence their speech and decision-making. The *LMX (Leader-Member Exchange) theory of leadership* underscores that leadership effectiveness hinges on these individual relationships rather than a uniform approach to all team members. This is true for individuals in family and society too.

In the epic Ramayan, Queen Kaikeyi paid heed to her most trusted maid Manthara's manipulative counsel to ask King Dashrath to make their son, Bharata, the heir to the throne of Ayodhya, instead of Ram, the rightful heir and the eldest son of Dashratha and his first queen, Kaushalya.

This request, fuelled by Manthara's advice, ultimately led to Lord Ram's fourteen-year exile, setting the stage for the epic's central narrative of duty, loyalty, and the triumph of righteousness. He was accompanied by his wife Sita and brother Lakshman. Amongst the many adverse consequences, the first was the plight of King Dashrath, who eventually died of grief.

In Mahabharat, Arjun sought guidance from Lord Krishna, while his cousin, Duryodhana turned to his maternal uncle Shakuni, a man known for his deceit and cunning nature, for advice. The wisdom and moral sense of Krishna let Arjun resolve not just an inner conflict but also emerge victorious in the war of Kurukshetra. The counsel from Krishna was steeped in righteousness and strategic brilliance. It exemplified the notion that where there is virtuous guidance, the way to triumph and the establishment of justice is never far behind. Contrary to Arjun's choice, through manipulation, evil planning, and malevolent strategies, Shakuni brought about the ultimate destruction and defeat of the Kauravas and the downfall of the lineage. The divergent roads each chose, one guided by wisdom and righteousness, and the other by crafty manipulation, ultimately led to the battle of Kurukshetra, one of the most gigantic epic wars fought in the history of mankind. This shows exactly how the wrong choices of guidance, guided by malicious intent, can even bring about a catastrophic end.

Another example is that of the great emperor, Chandragupta Maurya, the founder of the Mauryan empire in the Magadh kingdom of India. He was groomed by Chanakya, the counsellor and adviser to him. Chanakya steered Chandragupta from a mere boy to one of the mightiest emperors, proving that astute advice can take you to colossal heights. On the contrary, the fall of Roman Emperor Nero was largely due to him being influenced by corrupt and self-serving advisers. All this flawed leadership and flawed guidance had involved not only political instability but also a tragic end from bad decisions. These examples underline, even over time, a common truth: the advisers people choose will strongly determine their path and outcomes. Receiving the advice of such advisers not only places into view the bigness of the success, together with the vast legacy to be acquired, but also shows how deep integrity is rooted in the strategic acumen. There is a probability that failure and infamy are acquired when there is poor or unethical guidance in an individual.

Another way to look at the feeling of inadequacy is that not everything is wrong with Imposter Syndrome. A little dose of it can also become your saviour too! If self-doubt leads you to become a better learner, willing to work hard and open to new ways of doing things by turning *I don't know* into *I'll find out*, you're ready to up your leadership game. It even has a potential to become your powerful motivator and ally. Whether it's tackling unseen challenges or unleashing creativity when chaos strikes, it's about cultivating the idea of synthesising experience and learning to solve newer problems that life throws at you from time to time to test you. This mindset enables you to synthesise your past experiences and present knowledge to solve new challenges and to leverage your Imposter Syndrome. When you feel that your capability is greater than your confidence, it shows you are creating room for further growth and development. However, in the opposite case, when your confidence exceeds your competence, it can lead to complacency- one of the greatest hurdles to progress. In this sense, a small scoop of Imposter Syndrome helps you stay grounded with a flexible learning curve.

If someone says to you, *you're an idiot, the rest have it all sorted*, I bet you wouldn't like it. You will protest and express your reservations more if someone says this to your dear one. Why not treat yourself with the same love and respect without guilt when your mind starts playing the imposter game with you? Listening and giving importance to your inner voice when it gets into such monologues and self-deprecation mode needs a better treatment. The most crucial aspect here is to be able to learn that not everyone and everything matters all the time. Only a handful in life have your best interest at heart, be it at work, in your social circles, or within the family. You need to stop trying extra hard to impress everyone when you are already giving your best. Be focused on the areas of life that uplift you, like health, relationships, and learning. Stop feeling guilty about everything.

Some tips to manage your Imposter Syndrome are shared below.

1. ***Reframing:*** It is possible to turn your negative thoughts into positive opportunities. When you find yourself thinking, I'm not good enough, reframe it to, I am skilled and have unique abilities to handle it. Another example is, instead of thinking, I don't deserve this promotion, remind yourself, I was nominated due to the valuable skills and experience I bring to the table. Shifting your perspective from negative to positive self-talk can help you recognise opportunities in challenges and help you develop a realistic view of yourself. This cognitive switch can help treat mistakes as a part of the learning process and not as your report card of incompetence.
2. ***Success Journal:*** A journal in which you record your accomplishments, positive feedback, and compliments, will be your biggest Jambavant* to remind you of your power and achievements to boost your confidence during moments of self-doubt. The entries act as concrete evidence of your accomplishments, and going through them can boost your confidence through reinforcement of a positive self-image. Journaling will also foster a sense of reassurance to mitigate feelings of inadequacy and self-doubt.

   (*The reference here is to Jambavant in Ramayan, who reminded Hanuman of his power that the latter had forgotten due to a curse).

3. ***Seek Support:*** When you feel lost and directionless, turn to people who are professional and knowledgeable, like coaches, mentors, or counsellors. It helps in receiving guidance, objective feedback, and self-reflection to move forward when you are stuck. Consider issues related to relationships or careers. Opening up about your feelings or problems and figuring out the right direction with encouragement and support can help normalise feelings of Imposter Syndrome. Joining professional online communities to share your experiences and learn from others is another way to stay informed. There are zones of strengths and weaknesses. Build your moat and play the game based on your strengths. In the face of adversity, consider if it is possible to handle external threats with your innate strengths and even leverage them for survival and sustenance. If you cannot do it alone, can you turn to more knowledgeable sources that can assist you and make it less overwhelming? Capitalising on your strengths and being humble enough to seek help when needed will go a long way in your survival and sustenance.
4. ***Visualise Success:*** When you feel you are not ready, make the right effort and get into the mode of practising visualisation. You can imagine yourself succeeding in the challenging situations bothering you now to gain confidence and manage anxiety. For instance, before addressing thousands of people, you can practice and visualise yourself acknowledging the thunderous clap of the audience after doing it successfully. Practice will make you confident, and visualisation will nudge you to look forward to the desired outcome. The important thing here is to have a strong conviction to get into the action mode.
5. ***Set Realistic Goals:*** Making progress is important, but lofty tasks can often seem overwhelming. Being consistent and breaking down larger tasks into smaller, manageable goals are some of the ways to celebrate little milestones. If you wish to write a book, instead of trying to complete the entire book in a few days, you can write a minimum number of words each day to avoid boredom or burnout. Realistic milestones boost confidence in moving ahead with a balanced approach. Nailing each goal, no matter how small, reinforces your capability to conquer the next step ahead. You move

forward at a comfortable pace that gets gradually consistent and accelerated with the celebration of your progress.

6. ***Accept Compliments:*** In many cultures, modesty is valued so much that taking compliments is considered a sign of boasting or pride. Avoid downplaying your achievements as it may be treated as a sign of low self-esteem. Practice internalising positive feedback and compliments. When you dismiss compliments in your bid to show yourself as humble, the person complimenting you may feel awkward or confused. Not being able to accept a compliment can also point to Imposter Syndrome, which makes you feel you are not worthy of it. Start acknowledging when people praise you. It can be done with a simple folding of your hands in the *Namaste* position, or by saying, *'Thank you,'* with a smile.
7. ***Make Genuine Effort:*** Even if you're highly knowledgeable in your area of expertise, there will always be surprises—a sudden advancement in technology or a challenging situation at work or in your personal life—that might throw you for a loop. The only thing that's in your control is the mental readiness to accept the change and learn in line with your values and ethics. Flexibility is the key. It may seem like a task at first glance but developing the ability to adjust to new situations and seek assistance when needed is an important skill that can not only help you deal with self-doubt but also boost your abilities and self-assurance. Expertise isn't about having all the answers. It is about your openness to acquiring knowledge, adjusting, and advancing. Experiencing imposter syndrome may lead you to believe you should possess all the solutions but in reality, no one has all-encompassing knowledge
8. ***Be Flawsome:*** Making and normalising mistakes is part of the learning process. The focus should be on consistency and progress rather than perfection. What is crucial is to accept that you are human and not a machine churning out perfectionism every time. Mistakes must be treated as opportunities for reflection and learning, not for punishing oneself. What matters is getting up after falling. Start living by striving to find a balance between perfectionism and sloppiness.

Imagine this scenario. *You're at a get together. The discussion delves into a social concern that you haven't explored before. Instead of feeling awkward or feeling like being caught off guard, you could actively listen, pose insightful queries and afterwards delve into some research to grasp the subject better.* No matter how knowledgeable you may be, novel situations will crop up. Being adaptable and open to learning enables personal growth. It's not about having all the answers. It is about maintaining a mindset geared towards learning in any situation.

9. ***Self-Reflection:*** Just as your vehicle needs servicing from time to time, similarly, your growth trajectory needs servicing too. It needs to be revisited regularly to reflect on how you have grown over time and what else can be done to develop your skills for the future. This is immensely beneficial for not only reinforcing your sense of competence but also preparing you for the future, no matter, even if the progress seems small now. Seeking external validation may seem a thing of the past when you have the confidence to manage your path.
10. ***Name your Imposter:*** Imagine your imposter as a bothersome figure whose job is to plant seeds of doubt in your mind. Give it a name. Whenever you hear thoughts like, 'I am not capable enough,' or 'Soon, they'll see I am a fraud,' you can address them head-on as follows: '<Name of the Imposter>, why are you here again? Move aside, that's my place/job.' Naming your imposter helps you separate the thoughts of inadequacy from your true self that you'll be able to recognise when <name> is trying to take over the wheel. Just as you'd not let any uninvited person take control of your room, make every effort not to let your named imposter take control of your mind.
11. ***Six Thinking Hats:*** Instead of comparing yourself to others or following someone else's script, take a moment to reflect on what you truly want. Be proactive in steering your life and career by making decisions that align with your goals. Craft a narrative that reflects your unique journey. Here is a well-known tool for doing it, developed by a renowned psychologist, Edward de Bono, in 1985 called the Six Thinking Hats. He introduced the idea of parallel thinking, with six different "hats" to challenge each course of thinking the brain can

take. In these directions, the brain will consciously bring up different aspects of issues under consideration, such as gut instinct, sceptical views, or neutral facts. This can help in decision-making by balancing the rational with the emotional. Here is how it flows.

- ***White Hat (Factual):*** *It is like a blank slate that helps you collect facts and information on something. It stands for objectivity and neutrality (e.g., what are the facts available on this, current market trends, skills, industry-wise requirements?)*
- ***Red Hat (Emotional):*** *Considers feelings, emotions, and intuition (e.g. feeling or opinion about any issue, development, dilemma).*
- ***Yellow Hat (Positive):*** *Stands for considering the positive and constructive facets of the issue (e.g., advantages associated with job change, promotion, refusing or accepting something, new product, new location).*
- ***Black Hat (Critical):*** *This hat is the Devil's Advocate. It is about doing critical analysis and identifying challenges associated with the concerned area (e.g., potential obstacles, the hardest thing about something, problems, and difficulties).*
- ***Green Hat (Creative):*** *Donning this hat prompts you to be solution-oriented and think of creative and innovative approaches (e.g., creative solutions for handling organisational politics, skill development, and long-distance relationships).*
- ***Blue Hat (Thinking of the big picture):*** *It is about overview and represents an overall growth and development strategy. Thinking how to achieve clarity at each step and bringing in focus is the key here (e.g., what is the original plan and how can we stick to our agenda?).*

By 'wearing' and absorbing the essence of these hats, you can systematically approach your personal and professional development, ensuring a comprehensive and well-rounded strategy that considers various perspectives and aspects of your growth. A summary of the tool, with examples, is given below:

The Metaphorical Hat	Thinking Mode	Application to Handle Imposter Syndrome	Examples
White Hat	Information and Facts.	Review facts related to your achievements and feedback.	Look at the list of your successful projects, accolades, awards, and performance metrics.
Red Hat	Feelings and Emotions	Acknowledge and express feelings of inadequacy or negative self-worth.	Write or journal about your insecurities or feelings. Talk to a friend or professional.
Black Hat	Caution and Critical Thinking	Objectively identify areas for improvement.	Critically assess your skills, and plan for training.
Yellow Hat	Optimism and Positivity	Focus on strengths and successes.	Systematically list your accomplishments.
Green Hat	Creativity and Other Alternatives	Explore strategies that boost your confidence.	Visualise success, seek support through coaching, counselling, or mentorship.
Blue Hat	Process and Control	Develop a structured plan and monitor progress.	Set SMART weekly goals, keep a success journal, and review progress.

- What specific thoughts or feelings do I experience when I feel like an imposter?
- How do these thoughts and feelings affect my behaviour and performance in my personal and professional life?
- Can I identify any patterns or triggers that lead to feelings of imposter syndrome?
- How would I support a friend or colleague experiencing similar feelings of self-doubt?
- What evidence do I have that contradicts my negative self-beliefs?
- How can I reframe my thinking to acknowledge my skills, achievements, and worth?
- How do I typically respond to praise or recognition, and why?
- What actions can I take to seek support from mentors, peers, or professionals to address these feelings?
- What are some past experiences where I felt like an imposter but eventually succeeded? What can I learn from those experiences?

Chapter 6

Communication and Influence

(Image generated by DALL·E for Leadoscope)

Effective communication is the backbone of influencing. It is more than a plain exchange of information and certainly not just being fluent in a language. It is about making sense of underlying emotions and intentions behind verbal and non-verbal cues like body language. Communication needs to be clear to build trust and openness for ideas and relationships to flourish. Just as air is all around us, communication is the lifeblood that sustains and enriches every successful connection and interaction in family, society, or work. In organisations, the quality of communication shapes culture, teamwork, leadership, and public image.

Recall a situation.

Have you ever had a thought so strong you just had to speak up? At times, you may have felt overwhelmed and just reacted, only to regret it later. Expressing is cathartic, but doing it effectively is an art.

Oh, the power of speaking your mind!

However, it is not easy to observe restraint with so many polarising views that tempt you to react. You simply need to scroll through social media to spot such samples! Let's be real, sometimes our unfiltered thoughts are better left unsaid. The balancing factor is to find a way to share thoughts without being overly harsh or offensive.

The acronym CLEAR highlights the key tenets of communication.

C for Concise: A message must be communicated in a way that is easy to follow. Some people suffer from verbal diarrhoea and use bombastic language, which can be overwhelming for the listeners. Instead of giving a lengthy introduction or background to anything, stating things directly in simple terms is more impactful. Clarity is about distilling complex ideas into bite-sized, digestible, actionable messages that resonate with others.

An example is a direct and concise message as follows that can be supplemented with more details.

"We need to adjust our project timeline due to a shift in client requirements,"

L for Listening. Here, it implies listening to understand rather than to pass judgement. Active listening involves fully focusing on the speaker and understanding what they are saying. This is followed by repeating, if needed, to clarify, and thoughtful responses. Active listening helps in gathering rich and valuable insights and shows respect and appreciation for other people.

Some examples are given below.

"Do you mean to say______?"

"Just to make sure I understand, your concerns are________?"

"Just to make sure I understand, you're suggesting we prioritise learning over layoff for this quarter, correct?"

E for Exact: Here, the requirement is to be precise without being vague or ambiguous. Using specific, targeted language clarifies intentions and expectations, thereby reducing the risk of misunderstandings. This precision is needed to foster a better and more effective exchange of ideas, enabling the involved people to act with confidence and cohesion.

For example, if you need something by a certain date, you need to be straightforward and specify it.

Vague: *We need to get it done as soon as possible.*

Exact Communication: *This needs to be completed by next Friday, 5th May. It should include details about market research, an allocated budget for the next year, and a detailed risk assessment. Please ensure all sections are reviewed for accuracy before submission.*

Here, you present the information in a clear sequence:

- *A brief overview of why the change is necessary (client requirements have changed).*
- *What the new timeline looks like.*
- *How these changes affect current tasks.*

A for Authentic: Credibility in communication correlates directly to another essential aspect of influence: trust. Trust is the currency by which you do business. If your client or employee does not find you credible, they won't trust you, and it will be harder to influence them with your message. Before a meeting or presentation, do the necessary research to ensure that you are adequately prepared. Credibility for a communicator extends not only to what you say but also how you say it.

Example-

- **Colleague 1:** *Hey, do you have a moment to look at this report? I'm not sure if I've included everything asked by the manager.*
- **Colleague 2:** *Honestly, I'm busy right now and I won't be able to give it the attention you need. Let's plan a time later today so I can really help.*

Here, Colleague 2 is being authentic by sharing his limitations and giving a realistic option instead of rejecting the request or just going through the report for the sake of it.

R for Relevant: You focus on the important and relevant aspects, avoiding unrelated details about other project areas. Give constructive feedback to people to help them improve and grow.

Example: Your report was good. Let's work on adding some data to support the given points.

Here, you can effectively use storytelling. Connecting with people through personal stories that can convey your values and vision is always effective. For example: *When I started in this company, I faced a similar challenge. But with consistency, focused strategies, and collaboration, the team was able to overcome it.*

Effective communication is a two-way street. Engage people around you and be open to their feedback to create a culture of trust and collaboration. Much of the communication is non-verbal. Your body language, facial expressions, and even silence speak volumes. An important aspect is to understand that even silence speaks out aloud. Think about it. It is not to be mistaken simply as the absence of sound; it is a language in itself. Sometimes, silence can convey a variety of meanings and emotions that words cannot, thus providing scope for reflection and empathy. It can aid in fostering deeper connections. Active listening and thoughtful responses utilise silence effectively. Similarly, in negotiations, silence can be an extremely powerful tool. It can be a strong enabler of enriching communication and deepening connections between individuals by gauging even the unspoken feedback from others.

Leveraging Communication for Influence

Constructive feedback helps maintain open lines of communication and continuous improvement. Encourage and model how to give and receive feedback in a manner that is helpful and encouraging, not critical or demeaning. Different situations and people require different styles of communication. Leaders must be versatile, adjusting their communication style to best fit the audience and context, much like how air takes the shape of whatever it fills.

Influence comes from the ability to connect with people and align them towards common goals rather than mere authority. Effective communication helps in crafting compelling narratives that inspire action, motivate perseverance and instil a sense of shared purpose. You need to be cognizant of everything - what you say or don't say, what you show, and what you do. Being frank doesn't have to be without the application of the right organs. Speak your mind but be mindful of your body language too. If you say something, mean it. People can see through your façade most of the time.

Let's take the following examples to understand this better.

- *Supervisor 1: merely talks about safety rules with the shop floor workers in a detached manner without positive body language, like eye contact or posture, the workers might not take him or the instructions as seriously.*

  Contrast this with this approach

- *Supervisor 2: talking about the importance of safety from an empathetic angle, highlighting the need to stay safe to be there for the family and how the organisation supports all its workers and cares for their safety.*

The approachable stance in the second case will render more credibility and adherence to the safety rules.

- *Add to this another angle of a leader spending some time with the workers to show his genuine concern by inviting questions over a meal with them. The recipe for influence is right there, served on that table because communication meets the right intent here.*
- *Similarly, in a family setting, parents talking about the importance of good values like, honesty, integrity, and character, need to be truthful and authentic. If their actions do not match their intentions and sincerity is missing, it can send mixed signals to the children.*

When you are authentic and practice what you preach, people observe you and the message is driven clearly. The influence is much stronger in this case, reinforcing commitment to the values discussed. The more there is sync between words, body language, and actions, the more it cements influence and makes the world around you sit up and take notice.

1. ***Mirroring:*** This technique is about subtly imitating aspects like the gestures, posture, and eye contact of another person. Psychologically, it is believed to help in rapport-building due to a sense of familiarity and comfort. This is a widely used trick in negotiations and persuasion. It reflects the other person's behaviour non-intrusively and creates a sense of familiarity and builds a positive environment for communication. Mirroring is subtle and looks like paying attention to the speech pattern, gestures, pace, tone, body language, and postures of the other person to build rapport by matching the other person's energy without directly imitating their actions. For instance, during a conversation, if someone is speaking slowly, you can try to be slow when you speak. This simple adjustment can make the other person feel included and comfortable.

2. ***Role-Playing Scenarios:*** Regularly engage in role-playing exercises that challenge you to handle various communication challenges, from delivering difficult news to motivating disheartened team members, or being there for those in grief. Simulating real-life scenarios like handling customer complaints, giving feedback, and resolving conflicts enhances observation and problem-solving skills. Various communication strategies can be practised through role plays. Some key questions for the debriefing session can be:
    - *What did you find challenging about this scenario?*
    - *What would you do differently in a real-life situation?*

3. ***Communication Plan Template:*** Developing a template to plan your communications strategy for different audiences and objectives is handy and helpful. This should include key messages, delivery channels, timing, and feedback mechanisms. A sample is suggested below with various segments that a communication plan can include, along with examples for each.

Segments	Examples
1. Objective (The primary goal of this communication)	**Purpose:** Inform team of new project deadlines **Outcome:** Team members adjust their schedules accordingly
2. Audience (Identification and description of key audience)	**Primary:** Project team members **Secondary:** Department heads **Stakeholders:** Project sponsors
3. Key Messages (The core message that is to be conveyed)	**Main:** Deadlines have moved up **Supporting:** Reasons for change, new deadlines, expected workflow adjustments
4. Channels (List the channels to be use like email, social media, press releases)	**Primary:** Team meeting **Secondary:** Follow-up emails
5. Timing (Provide a schedule for when messages will be delivered)	**Frequency:** One-time announcement with follow-up **Schedule:** Next team meeting, immediate email afterwards
6. Resources Required (internal and external resources)	**Material:** Presentation for meeting, email template **Human:** Project manager for presentation, admin for email distribution
7. Feedback Mechanisms (Plan for collecting feedback)	**Direct:** Feedback form via email after the meeting/ action step **Indirect:** Monitor task progress updates

Segments	Examples
8. Evaluation (Evaluating the effectiveness of the communication effort through direct and indirect measures)	**Success Criteria:** Adherence to new deadlines, Key Performance Indicators (KPIs) **Review Process:** feedback from stakeholders, meeting reviews
9. Contingency Plans (Identify potential risks and mitigation strategies)	**Challenges:** Miscommunication **Mitigation Strategies:** FAQ document, open door for post-meeting questions

This template can be used for various personal and professional scenarios. Managing internal and external communication related to policies, people, products, and services; marketing campaigns; project management; crisis management; and organising events such as reunions and gatherings. Additionally, a communication template can be a brilliant support for social media campaigns.

4. ***Storytelling**:* Storytelling may be as old as the origin of mankind. It used to be in the form of visuals, such as cave drawings, before shifting to in-person conversations. Stories were passed down from one generation to another in the form of narratives. Connecting with your team through personal stories that can convey your values and vision is effective.

   Example: When I started in this company, I faced a similar challenge. But with consistency, focused strategies, and collaboration, I was able to overcome it.

   Each story can have a structure, be it oral or in presentation mode. Effective communication is a two-way street. The plot of a compelling narrative needs to be crafted carefully. Freytag's Pyramid is an effective framework to structure the plot of a narrative. Gustav Freytag was a 19th-century German playwright and novelist. He suggested a framework to show dramatic structure. There were seven parts to it, which have been shared in the template below:

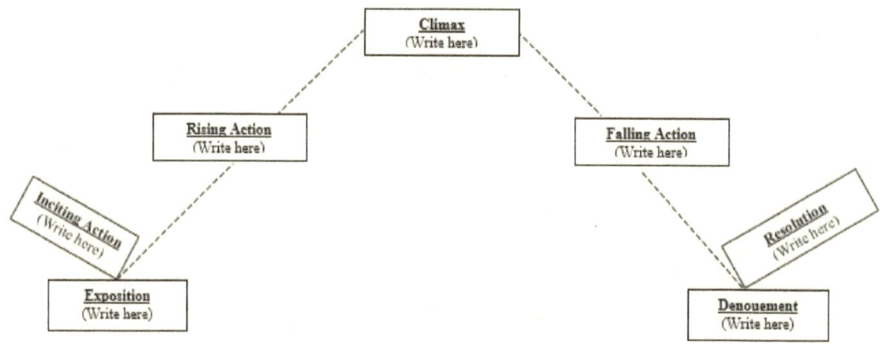

Figure 4: Freytag's Pyramid for Storytelling

- *Exposition (setting the scene by introducing the current situation and the need for change, if any).*
- *Inciting Action (any incident of importance that has set a chain reaction of events)*
- *Rising action (steps involved to progress and handle the challenges ahead)*
- *Climax (the crucial point where the action is at its peak, like the revelation of messages, intentions, decisions, etc.)*
- *Falling action (actions that follow the climax, sort of debriefing)*
- *Resolution (forward-looking towards the future after problem-solving)*
- *Denouement (happy or sad conclusion)*

A narrative can only be considered compelling when the audience can identify with it. Engaging people around you, be it your family, team, stakeholders, or anyone else, is a function of your body language and your narrative style. The exchange of ideas and openness to feedback create a culture of trust and collaboration. The Freytag framework will support you in giving a neat structure to your conversation, speech, or presentation. The applicability is vast, ranging from personal storytelling, public speaking, motivational talks, problem-solving discussions, and persuasive conversations to daily conversations with friends and family.

Multiple examples have been given below to serve as practical illustrations and enhance the clarity of explanations. These can be further elaborated with day-to-day instances of conversation related to feedback or explaining the importance of something. The following table explains this process with examples. You may use other examples to understand it better and restructure your speech and writing to make them more systematic, powerful, and emphatic. Good storytelling must have the right flow without much deviation from the core topic to maintain excitement. The narrative must bring in authentic emotions, supplemented by relevant anecdotes, as the story progresses. A powerful hook captures the interest of the audience and makes the transition flawless with a logical cascade of events. Portray how, at different moments, you (or the protagonist) experienced varied emotions like excitement, shock, anxiety, and even fear. This creates a connection with the listener, hence making the story more exciting and memorable.

Use a lot of vivid anecdotes that bring your story to life. Sharing relevant personal and professional experiences sets the stage for your audience. This will help to build the tension and anticipation of the story.

Sr. No.	Step	Example 1	Example 2
1.	Exposition	Hello everyone. As you know, our sales have been stagnant for the past quarter. Considering the market and our competitors, we need a fresh strategy to boost our numbers.	Lately, I've been feeling really stressed about managing my time between work and personal commitments.
2.	Inciting Action	The bad news is that last quarter, we lost a major client to a competitor. The team was highly disappointed and demotivated, but we treated it as a wake-up call.	Last week, I missed an important deadline because I was overwhelmed.

Contd...

Sr. No.	Step	Example 1	Example 2
3.	Rising Action	Some of us brainstormed and formed a task force. The tasks were assigned to study market trends and customer feedback. We developed a new sales approach, focusing on personalized service.	I've been researching time management techniques and found a few that seem promising. I've also started using a planner to organise my tasks.
4.	Climax	You will be happy to learn that just 3 weeks ago, we pitched our new strategy to another potential client. They were impressed and have agreed to sign a contract worth $1 million within 10 days.	Yesterday, I tried a new scheduling method and managed to finish all my tasks on time without feeling stressed.
5.	Falling Action	After this successful pitch, we trained the entire sales team on the new strategy. The overall feedback has been quite encouraging.	I plan to continue using this method and refine it based on what works best for me.
6.	Resolution	We are now optimistic about our growth because, after detailed analysis considering some calculated risks, we expect a minimum of a 15% increase in sales over the next quarter.	I feel more in control of my time now and less anxious about my commitments.

Contd...

Sr. No.	Step	Example 1	Example 2
7.	Denouement	Though we faced challenges, we adapted and succeeded. Let's continue this momentum and achieve our goals. Your role is instrumental because each one of you matters in this growth journey.	It's amazing how a few small changes can make such a big difference.

Effective communication is vital, yet often underestimated in its power to influence and lead. By mastering the art of communication, you can not only enhance your influence but also foster an environment of transparency and trust. As you breathe life with your words and actions, and sometimes even silence, remember the power of air: unseen, but essential, powerful, and all-encompassing.

Here is how a tightly-knit narrative can come together:

- Have you ever had one of those meetings where, after that meeting, you view everything entirely differently? *(Exposition with a strong hook)*
- I was having one of those problematic quarters last year, and I received a last-minute meeting invitation from the CEO. *(Inciting Action)*
- I felt anxious and a bit excited as I entered the room. Our company was going through rough times implementing a big project, and I had no idea what to expect. *(Rising action. Emotions.)*
- The CEO began the meeting by articulating his vision for our company's future in no uncertain terms and straightforward words. He talked passionately about our goals of innovation. And then he did something peculiar. He asked us for our ideas, no matter how far out there they seemed. I hesitated for a moment and then I shared a concept

that I'd been toying around with for weeks. *(Building suspense. The Climax. Emotions.)*

- I told him about an app, the idea for which came from deep frustration with another product. I remembered that afternoon quite vividly in the Summer of '69, navigating endless menus just to resolve a simple issue, and I thought we could do better. *(An anecdote, some humour, emotions)*
- Remarkably, he did listen to me and insisted that I work on that further. It has been a turning point. A small team was formed with the support of the CEO, and we worked very hard on the idea. *(Falling Action)*
- Months later, our project not only solved the initial problem, but also opened doors to new opportunities for the company. *(Resolution)*
- The experience taught me the value of speaking up and the impact of strong leadership. That was one massive lesson about collaboration and the power of innovation. Great ideas can indeed come from anywhere. *(Denouement)*

- ❖ How can I ensure my communication is clear and understandable to someone not familiar with the topic I need to discuss?
- ❖ In what ways can I improve my active listening skills during meetings and one-on-one interactions?
- ❖ What words do you use towards yourself? Will you use them towards others?
- ❖ How can you use words to lift yourself and others?
- ❖ What non-verbal cues do I commonly use, and how might these be perceived by others?
- ❖ How can I tailor my feedback to be more constructive, and less critical?
- ❖ How do I need to adjust my communication style when dealing with a crisis or conflict?
- ❖ How can I use a communication template for doing <task 1>, <task 2>, <task 3>…?

Chapter 7

Beyond Boredom: Embracing Possibilities

(Image generated by DALL·E for Leadoscope)

Congratulations if you're getting bored of routine, have hit a roadblock and things are increasingly getting monotonous. No hobby classes are helping, and you either feel like mentally murdering some people or leaving everything and meditating in the Himalayas.

Boredom is like an annoying itch. The more you scratch it, the more it bothers and satisfies you at the same time. The initial signs are a glance at your phone screen or tidying up your desk drawers. However, as it intensifies, you begin to observe details around you. Suddenly and unexpectedly, your mind grows weary of scrolling through familiar apps and begins to drift aimlessly. Like a bolt from the blue your thoughts are consumed by planning that book you promised to write, scheming up business ventures, or perhaps rearranging your entire living space on a Wednesday afternoon at 3 o'clock.

J.K. Rowling, the author of the Harry Potter series, shared that the idea for Harry Potter came to her in 1990 while she was on a delayed train journey from Manchester to London. As she was sitting in her seat, staring out the window, the idea of a young boy attending a school for wizards simply fell into her head. She did not have a pen and paper to write anything down. But the idea was so strong that she spent the rest of the journey mentally sketching out the characters and the story that would eventually become Harry Potter and the Philosopher's Stone.

This moment of inspiration during an otherwise mundane train ride was the spark that led to one of the most successful book series in history. Now, I am not proclaiming that boredom will necessarily lead to creativity. The emphasis is on the idea that you can start considering boredom in a new light and not make it the villain that it has become today for people to do just anything or everything for that quick dopamine rush without being mindful of the consequences.

Boredom has a message: *you need to revamp yourself.* It refuses to remain dormant. It pushes you until creativity emerges from its hiding place with reluctance and resistance. You will find that the boredom you feared transforms into a springboard for new thoughts and ideas. It is a push towards doing something, to make you feel better. The more the frustration, the greater the desire to overcome it. You are in an ideal position to create a fertile ground for creativity and magic by gravitating towards something that you can look forward to. This is possible through goal setting. Doomed or not without having your own goals, at least this thought is a rallying cry for self-awareness in our personal and professional lives! In simplest terms, it is a way to think along the following lines:

- *What do you want in life/career? If you don't know, think and reflect more with paper and a pen.*
- *Can you divide that goal into smaller, more achievable steps?*
- *Can you make those steps clear and measurable?*
- *Can you specify which daily tasks can help you move closer to that goal?*
- *Can you regularly review your progress honestly?*

In short, this is about the goals being SMART (Specific, Measurable, Achievable, Realistic, and Time-bound) for more clarity. Now, a pressing question is when and how will you do it.

The answer is simple. The sooner, the better, by reflecting and exploring ways to do it.

Let's say you are undergoing a mid-career crisis and are bored as hell at work. You're not alone. This common juncture can tempt you to think a new job will fix everything, which may or may not be true. Alternatively, you may wait for the organisation to change, which may not ever happen or at least not anytime soon. This can apply to personal life too. A sensible solution would be to work on oneself first. Before you look outward, you may consider looking inward. If you are not sure of your future, or what to do in life, simply focus on the next step.

Boredom will induce you to think more. In that process, you start considering newer ways to elevate your work and try alternate approaches to do the same things by encouraging new ideas, thus positively impacting the people around you. Improving these areas will not just enhance your current mindset; they'll equip you for better and more rewarding positions down the road. Possible to think over it?

This is how you can do it:

- *Identify one strength and one weakness in your work style.*
- *Set a small goal this week that plays to your strength.*
- *Seek feedback from someone who knows you well on how to improve your weakness.*

The key is to develop self-awareness. Without it, you don't truly grasp your impact on others, nor how they perceive you. Taking control of your narrative and ensuring your journey is defined by your dreams, not dictated by the aspirations of others, is crucial. You can focus on improving your current role and taking it to the next level. Instead of fixating on the distant future, concentrate on what you can do right now to excel in your current position. This change in perspective makes a significant difference. Enrolling in multiple skill development programmes in entirely new and unrelated areas can make you realise how other disciplines are not as distant as they seem; they are often interconnected with what you are already familiar with. It broadens your horizons and brings fresh ideas into your daily work.

The Einstellung Effect

There is an old saying - if the only tool you have is a hammer, you will start treating all your problems like a nail. There is beauty in diversity. What brings you to a point might not necessarily lead you to another! It is like that stubborn voice in your head saying, "I've always done it this way!" Understanding the Einstellung effect is useful in this context. Einstellung Effect was first methodically studied by Abraham S. Luchins in the 1940s. He performed a series of experiments to figure out how and to what degree past knowledge or experience influences problem-solving and decision-making.

Picture this:

You are guiding yourself or your team towards success, but Einstellung strikes to turn your back towards interdisciplinary knowledge and diverse thought processes. In short, you do not consider anything beyond what you have been doing. You fall into a trap of thinking what you have or what you know is enough. The need is to be a bit more. By questioning the typical and standard pathways, you can open new trails for exploration.

It pays to look for solutions in disciplines or trades different from yours. Often, techniques or methods from one field can be innovatively applied to another, providing fresh perspectives that lead to breakthroughs. When you indulge in finding out something new, boredom can be kept at bay. Bounded rationality helps when time and resources are limited, but rigidity in thought process due to fixation with older and familiar solutions, despite having better options, is alarming.

Like magicians, always learn something new to consistently challenge and surprise the audience with a new trick up your sleeve. Encouraging an innovative mindset and creating a culture where fresh approaches thrive are musts to navigate through unpredictability and boredom. Newer thoughts can be the greatest facilitators of your success. Growth isn't about being stuck in your ways but embracing new paths with a sparkle in your eye and saying, *let's see what you've got!*

Boredom also arises when you are faced with: *we've always done it this way; such things won't work here, we don't do it this way; we're doing it because others are doing it too; I know what I'm doing, don't need your revolutionary ideas.*

Press the reset button! Version 1.0 will not work in the era of Version 5.0 because it's a shield against innovation and hinders a growth mindset. If boredom leads to breaking free from the comfort zone and embracing change, it can be the fuel to survive and thrive. True leadership disposition is about fostering an environment where fresh ideas flourish like wildflowers. Let's be honest, the tried-and-tested paths may have brought you here, but the uncharted territories hold endless potential! Boredom arises when the mind seeks more and is not satisfied with the status quo.

When a team fearlessly debates between familiarity and forging ahead, that's the crossroad of progress and consistent action mode! Yes, some hearts and minds may face that jolt of 440V, but bring in a dash of courage, a sprinkle of wit, and voilà, there is no room for boredom!

But then, how do you know when it's time for that reset?

When you hear the whispers of untapped potential drowned out by the monotony of life; and, when possibilities knock louder than conformity, it is time to rally the troops and declare: we're pressing that reset button!

The ultimate solution to boredom is to think of this- the twinkle in the eyes of a child who has just begun to crawl or walk and is exploring everything around him/her. This trait starts dampening when the child starts growing up; that spirit of curiosity and enthusiasm starts fading, giving way to stress and compliance. As adults, to revive that sparkle, finding time to explore without treating it as compliance can reap rewards beyond imagination. In this context, the concept of neoteny can be a creative force to handle boredom. In biological terms, it refers to the retention of juvenile features in the adult stage of an organism. Neoteny was described in terms of an essential leadership trait by Warren Bennis and Robert J. Thomas in their famous Harvard article, *Crucibles of Leadership*. They described it as the ability to stay childlike in attitude, manner of response, and behaviour during a person's life and career with an attitude of curiosity, playfulness, creativity, and openness to new experiences. A strong sense of curiosity and a desire to learn, much like children explore the world with wonderment, allows one to always look for new knowledge, be adaptive, and be open to change—all elements that become crucial life skills in this fast-paced world.

Playfulness and innovation promote a culture of creativity with more risk-taking. Adaptability and openness enable them to manage through the complexities and uncertainties. Sometimes, this curiosity-driven exploration leads to unexpected 'aha' moments. Neotenic traits can be the creative force that turns boredom into an incubator for new ideas. When boredom becomes a green signal, it manifests itself as a prompt to explore, innovate, and grow toward sustained creativity and success.

I would like to use a simple idea here. *How do you fetch items kept on the topmost shelves in the kitchen or a closet that are supposedly beyond your reach?*

(Image generated by DALL·E for Leadoscope)

The following options are possible:

- *Elevate yourself, stand on tiptoes, and try to reach the item.*
- *Use a step ladder or ask a taller person to fetch it for you.*
- *Pick up a child in the house and raise him or her higher so that they can get it for you.*
- *Use a tool to bring the item to the brink of the shelf, and then get it.*

The above steps are, coincidentally, the same to grow in life. Compare the points below with the above-mentioned points.

- *Push your limits (Elevate):* When the traditional ways do not help, you try to raise yourself to reach a position or level.
- *Seek help (step ladder/taller person):* When you cannot do it by yourself and feel stuck, you can always turn to a coach, a mentor, or

anyone from whom you can learn, and that learning can guide you in the right direction.

- *Mentor others by helping them write their success stories (pick a kid):* When leaders beget leaders, when you help others grow in life, the reciprocal relationship goes a long way in fostering a sense of shared progress. It leads to the discovery of newer insights that you may not have realised existed within you.
- *Try out-of-the-box thinking to reach your target (tool):* Out-of-the-box thinking comprises treading beyond only the traditional or tried-and-tested solutions. It needs to explore alternative and unconventional strategies to solve problems or achieve goals, to uncover unique insights and innovative approaches that differentiate your efforts from the norm.

There is a fifth factor too.

Tell everyone in your style how you were able to reach the top to get what you wanted. For this, you need to use social media mindfully.

Boredom often leads to finding something new to give some exercise to your neurons. Every minute, changes are happening in the neural connections, which are responsible for learning and memory. It is known as synaptic plasticity. Help it remain flexible. When the brain receives and sends positive cues, its ability to function better gets boosted. The best part? It then works harder to re-discover that lost shimmer for you to make you feel more alive.

This can happen at any age.

Here are some practical tools and techniques to harness boredom into something creative and productive.

- ***Focus on What You Can Control:*** Rather than dwelling on an imaginative future where boredom does not exist, shift focus to your circle of control. You can only influence certain aspects of your life and career, and concentrating on these aspects can help you with acceptance. Change begins with a change in mindset. In the face of monotony, it's essential to find ways to grow, learn, and remain motivated. Laughing about your problems and making jokes about the situation also helps the mind perceive it as a non-emergency situation. If you're experiencing a similar situation, remember that thinking about change can be an opportunity for personal and professional growth. Embrace it with an open mind, and you'll be amazed at what you can achieve.
- ***Journaling:*** If you have not done it, it is time to give this humble experience a try. It can be a powerful way to express yourself without any filters. Daily writing can be therapeutic, and it can help you uncover creative ideas and self-reflections. Free writing can also turn boredom into a productive force when consistency starts yielding patterns and eureka moments for you. Going back to that writing years later is a throwback time of having captured moments in the past. It helps in transcending time and becoming a portal to your past self. It can also be a gateway to evolving perspectives, revealing growth and change

over the years, leading to a profound experience that, as you would recall later, was born out of boredom!

- ***Structured Downtime:*** In this age of constant scrolling and instant dopamine rush due to the easy availability of sources of entertainment at the click of a mouse, it pays to learn how to delay gratification to avoid a feeling of void post the dopamine rush. Boredom can also be avoided by learning how to enjoy oneself without the need to turn to external sources all the time. Incorporating periods of unstructured time can enhance creativity and problem-solving skills. Encouraging activities that require sustained attention without constant stimulation can lead to significant benefits. A simple activity, such as taking nature walks without any digital devices, can provide an opportunity for reflection and idea generation. Regularly scheduling time away from digital devices can help the mind become calmer.

When you're feeling bored out of your mind is when you tend to look for things to occupy yourself with the most. Boredom triggers a need for excitement and makes you lean towards activities that offer immediate satisfaction like scrolling through social media or watching videos. This urge for diversions is simply your brain's way of trying to combat the emptiness it is feeling by finding ways to keep busy. However, while these diversions may offer an escape from monotony, they could also hinder your ability to concentrate on important duties or engage in profound contemplation. If you're often experiencing boredom, remember that change begins with you. It can be an opportunity for personal and professional growth.

Embrace boredom with an open mind and redirect it towards creative forces. You'll be amazed at what you can achieve. Reimagining boredom as a positive force encourages a shift towards valuing downtime and introspection. As you move forward, embracing boredom can lead to richer, more creative and more fulfilling lives. By changing your perspective on boredom, you unlock its hidden treasure, transforming it from a source of discomfort into a wellspring of opportunity.

- When do I get bored?
- What specific situations or activities make me feel bored?
- What small changes can I make to manage boredom?
- What can I learn about myself from the times I feel bored?
- How can I apply these insights to future situations, to enhance my ability to manage boredom?
- How can I create more unstructured time in my schedule to allow for creative thinking?
- What new hobbies or interests can I explore to turn boredom into a productive outlet?

Chapter 8

Navigating Relationships

(Image generated by DALL·E for Leadoscope)

Forming meaningful relationships involves more than casual greetings, or shallow networking interactions like swapping business cards, or simply connecting online through social media platforms such as LinkedIn. It is about creating a deep sense of trust and respect based on genuine understanding and mutual interest in others motivations and obstacles to provide valuable support and insights that elevate relationships beyond mere transactions, to significant transformations. True networking entails being there for others not when you have a need but consistently showing up to provide support or share in their successes. Establishing these connections often requires going beyond norms and embracing empathy while connecting through shared experiences and vulnerability. When we genuinely invest in building relationships, with sincerity and a desire to witness the success of others, we form connections that're not only more potent and enduring but also deeply satisfying compared to simply exchanging contact details hastily.

Recently, I had a thought-provoking discussion with a more knowledgeable person. It had an interesting perspective about *treating someone you encounter as if that person were a postman delivering a letter*. This person can be anyone- your peer, your boss, your family, friends, acquaintances and even strangers. Sometimes, the message they bring is like a gift, that gives you joy and fills you with encouragement and positivity. It is heartwarming. However, there are other times when the message is not what you expected. It may have words that are difficult to digest, or even harsh and critical, casting a shadow of disappointment. It may hurt and disappoint you. But there is a profound lesson in all of this.

Just as a postman is not responsible for the content of the message, people are often the messengers of experiences and knowledge. Whether the message is delightful or challenging, it's essential to remember that we have the power to choose how we respond. We can use each message, regardless of its nature, as an opportunity for personal and professional growth. Practising it will help you to learn to appreciate the blessings, stay humble in the face of difficulties, and continuously evolve on your journey through life. Being open to the lessons that life has to offer in the form of encounters with various kinds of people, and their actions and behaviours will make you more resilient. The more you try to know people better, the better will be your understanding of human behaviour.

The best realisation is that the moment you have even an ounce of vanity about your deep understanding of human psychology, life will throw a new sample at you that you may have never seen or known. A new experience. Learning never stops. Networking helps in getting to know more people and the more you do it right, the better will be your learning.

When you attend a networking event or send out countless requests for connections on social media, it may not bear fruitful results if you are not mindful of curating your list and follow-ups. The power of soft networking helps to ace this game.

Networking is often seen as a numbers game, with the focus on accumulating as many contacts as possible. Investing your time in fostering genuine connections and getting to know the people behind the professional façade helps. By investing time and effort to understand someone's interests, goals, and values, you can better assess how your paths align and how you can support each other. Engaging in meaningful conversations, when possible, can help in delving beyond surface-level topics and allow for connections on a little more than simply a professional level. It may even go to a personal level.

Soft networking also promotes authenticity. When you genuinely connect with someone, you're more likely to be your true self, rather than putting on a façade to impress others. This authenticity fosters trust and strengthens relationships over time. However, it must be remembered that the most futile thing here is trying to be authentic because if you are authentic, you do not need to try. So, the next time, you know what to do. Ask people about their interests, hobbies, family, things that make them happy, their concerns, and their goals in life, and see the magic of the coolest spell you can cast. Keeping in touch and following up without any agenda is great for fostering deeper relationships. When people know that you value them beyond transactional interactions, they appreciate you more.

Leading self and others start with embracing vulnerability. It has the potential to impact the culture positively by creating a ripple effect in the organisation. Being a catalyst for a genuine, unstoppable wave of change starts with leaders. At the same time, if you show vulnerability, some people may struggle to accept it and might even distance themselves from you. Do not doubt yourself and your choice of being vulnerable. You are who you are and you need to change only for the better. It takes courage to be vulnerable and it takes more nerve to accept people as they are. Investing in relationships and growth with the right attitude and acceptance are non-negotiable in this process.

Here, it is important to note that your priorities must be clear. More than quantity, it's the quality of your connections that matters in life, and for that, you must be an explorer with some caution.

Some crucial reflections can be as follows:

- *Not everyone would be open to fostering deeper connections but then do you want everyone in your circle?*
- *How selective or open should you be about including people in your circle, or being included in theirs?*
- *How do you need to curate your circle? Careful consideration, spontaneous encounters or a mix of both?*
- *How can you deal with someone who is turning out to be a disruptive factor in your life?*

On 15th March 44 BC, Julius Caesar was betrayed and assassinated by one of his closest allies, Brutus. A seer had warned Caesar to be cautious on this day, and soon after when Caesar thought he was safe (as the day had almost already passed), the assassination happened before the day could end completely. There are so many lessons in this episode, starting with trust. It highlights the importance of choosing allies wisely. It also underscores the need for open communication to prevent misunderstandings and unbridled dissent. Managing relationships is about understanding the undercurrents and adjusting to the fragility of power dynamics. Prioritising trust-building in the team is crucial, and so is creating more allies. Value people who are not afraid to differ. They do not compromise on their values and will protect their ideals and principles at all costs. They are not yes-people but those who value the ideals and principles. Listen to them. Give credit where it is due. *If you are betrayed, use it as an opportunity to learn and grow as a person (it's only applicable to those alive). Always be vigilant.*

Betrayal doesn't mean people shouldn't be trusted. Trust people but change your yardstick to learn whom to trust, and that can only happen when you trust more. You gain newer experiences and wisdom to filter the people who truly matter.

Strategic thinking, along with a good understanding of people and relationships, is needed for your growth and development. The more you learn, the better your analysis of people's personalities and what motivates them towards doing something will be. An interesting fact is everyone is motivated; you just need to find out what motivates them. Some chase external markers of success, while others consciously focus on finding joy in cultivating growth and relationships. Redefining the essence of relationships is necessary here because a few quick doses of dopamine achieved through social media or fame can never be long-lasting. To find a deeper sense of fulfilment and joy, both at the personal and professional levels, reflecting on what constitutes your circle is key. I have seen people running after external validation from others and ending up with high levels of stress and anxiety. In the hustle and bustle of crafting networks, it helps to pause and ponder if we are building bridges or just seeking stepping stones. Many people like to be associated exclusively with those who can benefit them in one way or the other. Some others understand the true essence of collaboration—where mutual growth and shared success flourish. This is a rare segment.

Positive interactions can boost your immune system and overall well-being because the feel-good factor around it either makes you feel happy, inspired, or both. You end up stimulating the happy hormones in your body.

Maturity is when you realise that the quality of your relationship matters, and you start developing more meaningful relationships with the few people who make a difference for you. When you choose to surround yourself with people who lift you rather than drag you down, it profoundly impacts your quality of life. It creates a positive change in your mindset through increased drive, mental clarity, and a sense of serenity. The cumulative influence helps in driving you toward your goals as you navigate challenges with greater resilience and reduced stress. Similarly, by choosing to be the one who radiates a positive aura, you can create a nurturing and empowering atmosphere for others. Relationships must promote personal growth and happiness and make you feel good about yourself. If this does not happen, it is crucial to reassess the inherent dynamics. Negativity of any kind, like unhappiness, insecurity, or anxiety, needs to be examined. In such cases, open communication, seeking external support, or even considering ending the relationship may be necessary steps to ensure that both individuals can thrive and pursue their personal development and happiness. In these circumstances, open communication, external help, or even contemplating ending the relationship are key steps if both parties are to be true to themselves and pursue their developmental happiness.

A wonderful part of getting older is that you may develop clearer filters. After a lifetime of holding back, it becomes relatively easier to speak your truth. You learn that there is no benefit to hiding your authenticity. It creates a wonderful chance to challenge the norms, if needed, and cultivate a network built on trust, reciprocity, and collective prosperity. The world needs more than just transactions; it craves empathy, understanding, and collaboration. In a realm where connections often lean towards self-interest, can you redefine the narrative?

1. SOFT framework (For soft networking)

Acronym	Step	Description	Actions	Reflections
S	Show interest	Show sincere interest in others' lives and careers.	Ask open-ended questions. Listen actively	How do I feel after interacting with this person? (Interested and engaged, or obligated and disinterested?)
O	Offer value	Offer help or resources without expecting immediate returns.	Share useful information. Offer support or assistance.	Do I feel that my contributions and support are valued and appreciated, or do I feel taken advantage of and unappreciated?
F	Foster relationships.	Keep regular, light-touch contact to sustain relationships over time.	Send occasional messages. Schedule periodic check-ins.	Do I feel happy and uplifted after spending time with this person, or do I feel drained and stressed?
T	Travel and explore	Use travel as an opportunity to meet new people in unexpected places.	Engage with fellow travellers, and attend festivals and events beyond your industry and usual interests.	Have my interactions with new people brought positive experiences and growth, or have they introduced negativity and disruption?

(Source: Author)

2. ***Johari Window:*** A well-known framework that is often used for developing communication and self-awareness skills can be effectively used for networking, right like a pro. The Johari Window Framework was developed by American psychologists Joseph Luft and Harry Ingham in 1955. The name Johari was derived from the first few letters of each name. This framework consists of 4 quadrants that are interpreted on the X and Y axes. The X-axis is information about the self that is either known or unknown to the self. The Y-axis is information about the self that is either known or unknown to others. The details of each quadrant are given below.

   i) ***Open Area (Arena):*** In this quadrant, information about the self is known both to you and the others, hence the name. While networking, when you can be open and authentic about yourself, it builds trust, and others find it easier to connect with you. The objective in this quadrant is to either ask or tell to expand this zone. For instance, you can update your LinkedIn profile and share useful and informative content. It will not only reveal your professionalism but also your personality when you regularly engage in conversations and create value for people's time and focus. In in-person meetings, your smile and body language must come across as positive and sincere for people to open up with you and invite you to share more with them. When you are genuinely interested in others' skills, interests, experiences, and narratives, you invite them to be more open, and in turn, they too reciprocate well.

   ii) ***Blind Area*:** this quadrant is about aspects that others can observe or already know about you, but you don't. Consider this. You wish to improve your digital footprint and make it impressive. At the same time, you are running short of ideas on how to do it. Here, you may seek feedback from others, especially experts. To gain an understanding of how others perceive you, you can request feedback or indulge in detailed conversations and make notes about yourself objectively.

   Listening and being open to constructive criticism will help in removing the blind spots.

iii) ***Hidden Area (Façade):*** This quadrant focuses on the information that you know but others don't, and that is why it is called hidden. When you share some personal stories, views, and opinions, and sometimes even your state of mind, it will help in fostering deeper connections with people. Selectively sharing relevant personal anecdotes, experiences, and insights about your professional life can help in reducing the hidden area by making you come across as someone approachable.

Oversharing may backfire. A balanced approach has the potential to create magic.

iv) ***Unknown:*** Here, the information about you is unknown both to you and others. For example, neither of you would have any idea how you would perform in a new role that was handed over to you during a crisis when no other substitute was available. You may do exceedingly well or falter. Time will tell. For networking, it translates to exploring new learnings, experiences, and connections to assess if there are hidden talents and interests that can be unearthed.

Engaging with diverse people and activities from various cultures and nationalities on forums or cross-industry events, participation in new projects, and moving beyond your comfort zone can lead to unexpected experiences, lessons, and opportunities.

The central idea is that opening up is good for your relationships, and it grows when you engage in 2 things:

(a) Asking: meant to be inquiry, listening, and absorbing.

(b) Telling: arouses more candour.

Given below is a summary of the Johari Window framework that has been used here for networking.

You may substitute the suggested examples with what works for you.

	Known to Self	**Unknown to Self**
Known to Others	**Open Area**	**Blind Area**
	• Highlight the aspects you want people to value and remember you for.	• Seek feedback
	• Discuss openly in networking events.	• Ask for insights during interactions.
	• Showcase whatever you wish people to know about you in your professional profile.	• Use feedback for improvement.
Unknown to Others	**Hidden Area**	**Unknown Area**
	• Gradually share personal insights and stories.	• Explore new experiences and roles.
	• Use these to create deeper connections.	• Engage in continuous learning.
	• Reveal traits during appropriate opportunities.	• Seek diverse networking opportunities.

If you are worried about being judged, shamed, or given a cold shoulder, you need to remind yourself that you have nothing to lose. Work more on your confidence and trust yourself. Discloseonly as much as is required to get the conversation going. Go ahead and ruminate over these questions for your growth.

- What steps should I take to be ready to connect more with unknown people?
- How can I identify with whom to connect and how?
- What steps can I take to demonstrate my own trustworthiness to others?
- How can I better understand the motives of people?
- What are the advantages and disadvantages of this connection?
- What signs should I look for to understand if the person I have connected with is,
- How can I improve my skills to:
    - ensure clarity and prevent misunderstandings in my relationships?
    - establish and communicate boundaries clearly?
- Who can support me to handle a conflicting situation?

Chapter 9

Mindset Mastery: Beyond Success and Failure

(Image generated by DALL·E for Leadoscope)

Bob Marley said, "Some people are so poor, all they have is money."

A fulfilling life cannot be contained in a QR code. The things that genuinely matter in the long-term are the ones that can be felt or cherished and not necessarily scanned or measured. The role of one's mindset is the pivot around which most actions revolve. Mindset is the way you think and feel about yourself and the world around you. It influences how you perceive and approach challenges, problems, and decision-making. Your mental attitude also impacts how you react. Your past conditioning is a repository of your experiences that shaped your behaviour. Learnt behaviour can be a catalyst as well as a limiter of your future conduct and potential.

Let me share a true incident that explains the importance of understanding how one's mindset may be shaped by past conditioning.

The car cleaner rang the bell.

I opened the door.

He asked for the car key and I handed it over to him. I complained that he was cleaning the car well but not my two-wheeler (a scooty) and demanded to know why. He seemed a bit surprised and said, *I did clean it yesterday!*

Me: *But you didn't ask for the key. How can you say that you cleaned it?*

He: *Madam, why would I need keys to clean a scooter?*

There was a moment of silence interrupted by my laughter. The car cleaner smiled too. I had bought a scooty for the first time in my life. I was used to the cleaner asking for the car keys every second day to clean the interior, like the seats and the mats. When he didn't ask for the key for my two-wheeler even after 5 days since I bought and stationed it in the parking space, I blamed him for not cleaning it.

It was truly a facepalm moment. My past habit had conditioned me to expect the cleaner to ask for the keys every second day, and it had become a pattern that I began to rely on. My mindset was shaped by this predictable pattern. I had developed an expectation that for the vehicle to be cleaned thoroughly, the cleaner had to be given the keys. This expectation influenced how the current situation was interpreted. When my conditioned expectation was not met, based on my mindset, I easily concluded that he had not cleaned the scooter and blamed him.

Isn't this true in life, too?

- *When opinions and judgements are based on past experiences and assumptions,*
- *When people fail to adapt to new situations or changes in the environment,*
- *When you are in your ivory tower and fail to see the reality that is obvious to others.*

Success and failure are often attributed to one's efforts, circumstances, and a dollop of luck, or a lack of it. At the same time, a deeper understanding of the mindset and past conditioning does shape your perceptions and associated reactions. The intricacies involved here can give you valuable learning from achievements and setbacks that you can turn into building blocks for resilience and personal development.

The world today spins on a mirage of being comfortable with a false sense of security. You plan based on predictable pieces of life. *If I die, my insurance will cover this cost; if I lose my job, I have savings to support me for 6 months; if I wish to retire at 40, my financial corpus can take care of it, and so on.* Much of the predictable planning for life is done based on the known-knowns, as well as the known-unknown pieces (e.g., death or events that you have not experienced). When, without warning, a Black Swan emerges as an unforeseen event (unknown-unknown) with profound consequences, it compels you to view things, people, relationships, and events in a new light with new lenses. The mindset of taking things, relationships, positions, and power for granted can topple the strongest and the mightiest! This term was first used in 2001 in the context of finance by Nassim Nicholas Taleb, a finance professor, writer, and former Wall Street trader when referring to events that are outliers with extreme impact.

Uncertainties and disruptions have reshaped people, industries, and societies since time immemorial. The Black Swan theory teaches you that the unpredictable is always lurking. It's a call to embrace uncertainty, to be agile and adaptable, and to constantly challenge our assumptions.

Learning to thrive in the face of the unknown is a testimony to helplessness as well as resilience. When the future is full of surprises and uncertainties, problem-solving and decision-making assume greater importance as critical components in life. The way you approach challenges around these significantly impacts your survival and sustenance. As disruptors, the Black Swans are also a reminder of the strength of human adaptability and the importance of cherishing the known and the constants in your life.

The prudence in making sense of success or failure lies in an objective analysis of outcomes. When you learn from experiences and adapt your actions accordingly to move ahead, you understand that success or failure is a part of your journey, and the definition of each varies from person to person. Life needn't be linear or straightforward. It's prudent to stop occasionally to review what you're doing and if it's making any sense to you. When does one take a giant leap forward? Multiple scenarios work here, some of which are listed below.

- When the person has everything and nothing left to prove,
- When the person has nothing left to lose.
- When you are feeling stuck and suffocated,
- When you wish to outdo yourself,

By reflecting on the factors that work and the ones that don't, you can formulate a realistic picture of your goals. Doing a 360-degree examination of the current situation and the action needed to reach the desired situation is desirable, along with good health for standing tall in the face of perceived failure or success! Being resistant to change and applying outdated or ineffective tactics will not only hinder your growth but also make it difficult to adapt to new environments. You will also not be able to take advantage of the emerging trends. Introspecting on life & career is the core of personal and professional development. Action mode is paramount in this expedition ahead. Your brain cells love good workouts, so flexing them is not a choice but a compulsion for neuroplasticity. To learn something new acts as the rhythm for the mind that starts swaying to its beats, like a dancer in perfect sync! Upgrade your skills more than you upgrade your gadgets or wardrobe. A fancy degree and diploma are fine for a job, but what about the superpowers that you miss if you stop challenging your limits? Elevators can't take you everywhere. To soar higher, you need the rocket of relevant and upgraded skillsets. The job market is exciting as well as scary, so it's always better to be ready with ever-evolving skills instead of lamenting at the unpredictability of external factors. Relying only on your present job or business is fine if you are confident with this question - *can I manage if I wake up tomorrow without this job or business? Can I sustain comfortably for the next few months? Year?*

Success often shines with glory, but it's your failures that carve the path to wisdom and growth. In each failure, it is possible to discover the unexpected stepping stones on your journey to a sense of fulfilment!

You can learn 5 amazing things from your failures when you reflect on the following mindfully.

1. ***Identifying Passions and Pursuits (The Streak of Creation): What do I love and can pursue with more effort?***

- **Objective:** Identify activities or areas that you are passionate about and where you have a natural streak of creativity.
- **Action Steps:**
    - Reflect on moments where you felt most engaged and enthusiastic.
    - List activities or tasks that sparked your creativity and joy.
    - Plan to allocate more time and resources to these activities.
    - Set specific goals to improve skills and outcomes in these areas.

2. ***Recognising Strengths and Interests: What I like and can pursue with some effort?***

- **Objective:** Identify activities or areas that you enjoy and are relatively good at, though they may not ignite the same level of passion.
- **Action Steps:**
    - Reflect on tasks that you perform well and enjoy to a reasonable extent.
    - List these activities and evaluate their potential for growth and improvement.

- Develop a plan to invest a moderate amount of effort in these areas.
- Set achievable milestones to track progress and improvement.

3. ***Acceptance of Necessary but Unpleasant Tasks: What I don't like, yet need to accept?***

- **Objective:** Recognise tasks or responsibilities that are essential despite being unenjoyable.
- **Action Steps:**
    - Identify tasks that are necessary for personal or professional growth but are not enjoyable.
    - Reflect on the reasons why these tasks are important and unavoidable.
    - Develop strategies to make these tasks more manageable (e.g., breaking them into smaller steps, finding ways to minimise discomfort).
    - Cultivate a mindset of acceptance and focus on the long-term benefits.

4. ***Elimination of Unnecessary Dislikes: What I don't like and can eliminate?***

- **Objective:** Identify activities or tasks that are both unenjoyable and unnecessary.
- **Action Steps:**
    - Reflect on tasks that you dislike and that do not add significant value to your goals.
    - List these activities and assess their impact on your productivity and well-being.
    - Develop a plan to eliminate or delegate these tasks.
    - Free up time and energy for more valuable, and enjoyable pursuits.

5. ***Adapting to Unpleasant but Necessary Changes: What I don't like, yet need to adapt to?***

- **Objective:** Recognise areas where adaptation is required, despite discomfort or dislike.
- **Action Steps:**
  - Identify changes or tasks that are necessary, but currently uncomfortable.
  - Reflect on why adaptation is important for growth or success.
  - Develop strategies to adapt to these changes, such as seeking support, acquiring new skills or changing your approach.
  - Set small, incremental goals to ease the adaptation process.

Those who dare to fail at multiple things with a never-say-die spirit and can think on their feet are the ones who eventually win big! It needs agility, humility, and willingness to learn from each experience.

Organisations, leaders, parents, and teachers need to encourage a culture in which failure is not a taboo! Where people experiment to innovate, are not afraid to take calculated risks, embrace setbacks as stepping stones towards success, and where resilience is celebrated as a key ingredient in the recipe of progress and growth. In such an environment, creativity soars, innovation thrives, and the potential for ground breaking achievements becomes limitless. The definition of success is subjective, and so is that of failure. Your mindset determines which aspect you choose - the one laid down by society or the one that you will craft for your unique journey.

The interpretation of success or failure varies from person to person and is subject to individual perspectives, values, priorities, and goals. For some, a high-ranking and well-paying position that involves slogging day and night is synonymous with success, while for others, it may be perceived as a total failure in not being able to balance the scale of personal and professional life. Some associate success or failure with external validation, while for others, internal validation and satisfaction define success. For some, working through multiple all-nighters may constitute success, while for others, it might mean getting a sound, full-night sleep.

What matters are your priorities in life and how much you are willing to be content with. How you carry on and what lessons you learn from your chosen interpretation of success or failure will shape your learning path.

Are you shaping your life and career the way you'd like to?

You may have complaints against people and work. Either you can try to fix everyone and end up feeling more hopeless, or you can recognise that you cannot change others. What can be changed is your lens. The wisdom lies in working on yourself so that you stop being affected negatively and channelling your emotions for the right cause. Change is inconvenient, and even more so when it is a script playing in your head, conditioned by experiences and influences from your childhood to date.

Whatever your dream is, the outline to materialise it exists. Think of it. Someone else is already following it in some corner of the world, but instead of just going through the motions or following someone else's script of success or failure, take a moment to reflect on what you truly want. Discover and identify your metrics of success, and then concretise them through the right action.

Every decision and choice you make will shape you and your life. The scriptwriter in you needs to wake up, pull up your socks, and pick up a pen to write a story for the world that only you can tell – a story that is uniquely yours, filled with your priorities, insights, emotions, and experiences, waiting to inspire, challenge, and connect with others. Imagine your life as your favourite show and you're the one in charge. Focus on the goals that truly matter to you—whether it's learning new skills, pursuing your hobbies, or building real connections. Take small steps forward as a chance to add a new scene or plot twist that enriches your story.

In the end, your life will reflect the choices you made, the lessons you learned, the experiences you embraced, and how you made others feel. It is all about the overall impact you had on others.

Success and Failure Template

Step 1: Define Success and Failure

1. What does success mean to you? Clearly state your visualisation of it.

2. What constitutes failure for you? How do you deal with it?

Step 2: List Major Successes and Failures

Create a table in a spreadsheet or in your diary to evaluate your major perceived successes and failures over a specified period. You may include details and modify the table below. You may modify the table by adding more rows and columns.

Date	Goal/Event/ Project	Success or Failure	Description (What Happened?)	Takeaways, Reframing
2024-08-6	Publish a book	Failure	Unable to complete even a chapter.	Need consistency in reading and writing.
2025-01-20	Fitness goal	Success	Achieved a personal best in the marathon.	Consistent training, healthy diet, and mental resilience
2025-12-21	Qualify for a national-level entrance exam and get admission to a top institute	Failure	Scored 85th percentile and struggled in Quant.	Need to focus on other exams and try for admission in a top international institute.

Step 3: Analyse Patterns and Trends.

1. What factors do you feel helped you succeed? Be specific.

   ____

   ____

2. What obstacles or issues led to the setback? Are these recurrent or one-off hurdles?

   ____

   ____

Step 4: Reflect

1. What did you learn from your success?

____

____

2. Reflect on the lessons you learned from your failure.

____

____

Step 5: Revisiting Your Goals and Action Plans.

Based on your appraisal of the reasons behind success or failure, do the following.

- Set new specific, measurable, achievable, relevant, and time-bound (SMART) goals, and create action plans that align with your values and aspirations.

Goal 1:

- ***Description:*** ______________________________

- ***Action Plan:*** ______________________________

Goal 2:

- ***Description:*** ______________________________

- ***Action Plan:*** ______________________________

- What are my measures of success?
- What are my measures of failure?
- What external factors influence my perception of success or failure?
- What are my core values and how do they align with my goals?
- How have my past failures contributed to my growth?
- What does success look like to me on a personal and intrinsic level?
- What skills or behaviours consistently lead to my successes?
- What areas do I need to improve to avoid recurring failures?
- What do I want in life?

Chapter 10

Dilemma and Decision-making: Filtering the Noise

(Image generated by DALL·E for Leadoscope)

Living beings perceive external stimuli first as threats as a part of evolutionary conditioning that makes them react in milliseconds via the fight, flight, or freeze modes. This would have worked had human beings still been in caves, hunting around for food and existence. The basic needs today are more about empowerment than sustenance and mostly do not create a state of emergency unless in situations like wars and calamities. This means giving in to the habit of treating most tasks and challenges as urgent and assigning them an emergency status can backfire. The understanding that not everything needs an immediate response helps you distinguish between real exigencies and routine matters. When you start mixing up the two and start neglecting the sustaining aspects of your well-being, such as proper diet, rest, hydration, regular physical workouts, leisure time, and time with family and friends, it can impact your health and relationships negatively.

If years ago, someone would have told you the price of freedom when you started earning your own money to be independent in the future, you may have laughed it off. You realise it today when you ask your family to wait, be considerate, and adjust all the time because of your work, your habits, office culture, or policies. They understand. Yet again. You justify your acceptance, indulgence, or avoidance, and convince yourself by using lame arguments. You know the importance of proper sustenance, yet your hectic lifestyle often leads you to ignore these needs. You wonder how much the economy and your bank balance are growing, but the hearts of families are shrivelling. Advancing age and lack of quality time with family on the one side, and demanding work schedules, expectations, layoffs, fear of unemployment, rising costs of living and education hovering over it all on the other are leading to immense stress, and people are ageing before time. This dissonance can manifest as stress, guilt, or rationalisations that further undermine your well-being.

You realise you are neglecting your health and relationships, or doing something unethical or wrong, and still defend your actions when confronted with the possible outcomes of the situation.

Why?

The answer is self-justification.

Leon Festinger, a psychologist, explained this phenomenon he called *Cognitive Dissonance.*

It is a protective mechanism that helps you to see what you want to see, hear what you want to hear, and ignore everything else that is contradictory to your views. It works in the situations mentioned above. The neglect often creates psychological discomfort experienced when your actions contradict your values or beliefs. One of the most well-known examples here is when someone continues to smoke despite seeing and ignoring the warning on the cigarette packet.

You have two options to overcome this dissonance.

- *You can either change the action (I will not do this because it's not right for me or the others), or,*
- *You may change the belief (I will keep doing it because it's okay, everybody does it).*

To resolve this cognitive dissonance, it's essential to align your actions with your understanding of the importance of what sustains you. Prioritising a balanced diet, regular exercise and sufficient rest can help reconcile the gap between our knowledge and behaviour. By treating the basic foundation with the importance it deserves, you can build a strong basis for overall health and productivity, reducing the mental strain caused by cognitive dissonance.

Taking care of your basic needs is not just about survival; it's about empowering yourself to lead a more vibrant and effective life, free from the internal conflict that arises when you neglect the roots. A simple act, such as smiling, gives a signal to your brain to start releasing feel-good chemicals. It is for the same reason that activities like exercising, watching comedy, having good food, a change of scene, talking to positive people, and some quality break from the hustle and bustle of life can significantly improve the quality of your emotional well-being. You may often find yourself reacting to things in ways that could have been avoided.

Now the good news.

What you experience is common, driven by your natural response to trigger-generating situations or states of mind like stress, anxiety, frustration, or fear. These reactions are often impulsive and cloud your logic. Decision-making may be clouded because of these precursors that do not serve your best interests. To navigate ahead with grace, you need to train the logical part of your brain to keep the responses within your control. When you train for this, it requires you to begin with awareness of your triggers as the first step towards change.

In 1995, Daniel Goleman developed the idea of Emotional Intelligence, a concept introduced by American psychologists Peter Salovey and John Mayer in 1990. It is a skill that involves evolving the ability to comprehend and manage emotions to be able to utilise them effectively. This involves training distinct regions of the brain associated with emotions to be mindful about how to respond. Biologically, the human brain is a complex organ having billions of interconnected neurons and neural pathways. It plays a crucial role in regulation and decision-making, along with prepping you for relationship management, self-awareness, and self-regulation.

Picture this. Even though sometimes you feel like you make decisions consciously, that is not the case. You may have taken the decision already before 'actually taking it'. Neuroscientific studies in sports interestingly revealed that decisions are made within milliseconds. Examples are driving, catching a ball, or even online consumer behaviour. Interestingly, these decisions are driven by the subconscious mind. Over 95% of the decisions you make happen without you being aware of it. It's like the brain has this powerful autopilot mode to drive everything around. Only a tiny part of your brain's processing capacity, about 0.0005%, works at a conscious level. The rest, 99.9995%, is handling decisions without you consciously knowing. Little wonder then when you ask for advice, you're sometimes actually seeking validation for what's already there in the mind, albeit at a subconscious level. This has strong implications.

In his book "The Hidden Brain," Shankar Vedantam highlights a massive transformation in understanding human behaviour and likens it to a paradigm shift. He emphasises the need for fundamental changes in existing research methodologies and communication strategies. It pays to work on your subconscious mind so that your biases and notions do not act as major negative barriers in your or someone else's life. Getting over rigidity and having the humility to learn new things are keys to an agile mindset. Mastering it will help you manage emotions too. The focus is to strengthen your prefrontal cortex, which is associated with rational thinking and restraint.

The restless or unbridled mind is like a monkey, hopping from one tree to another. You must learn how to hold the reins and run the show. Your choice of action in dealing with dissonance will design the path ahead. The road not taken will make all the difference.

Positive or negative, the choice is yours!

To develop awareness, reflect on the following questions.

- *Do I reflect on why I react the way I do?*
- *What events trigger my emotions?*
- *Do I verify facts before forming conclusions?*

The right leadership disposition hinges on being open to new information and possibilities that may be obvious to others but not to you. Be willing to adjust expectations. Avoid making assumptions and instead seek to understand the current situation. In the face of any dilemma, either flip a coin if that is what helps you with decision-making or ask yourself the following 2 questions to enable you to, reflect on the current situation with thoughtful alternatives without getting into a mindset of justification. You will not fall into the temptation of emotional reaction and will logically think over it on two parameters.

- *What factors are holding me towards it?*
- *What is pulling me away from it?*

When you learn to recognise your emotional patterns, it is time to channelise them. The way you respond to events will influence the outcomes.

Factor in this example.

Just like you use money to purchase your house, you have invested your time and energy in the past for being and continuing in your comfort zone in the present (e.g., job, organisation). The predictability associated with it - both good and bad - is comforting to you because you know it inside out. The sense of security, complacency, or the desire to cling to power that you have garnered over the years in a known set-up are other factors that keep you where you are. The risks and anxieties you associate with the world beyond your zone do not let you take the plunge. At the same time, everyone doesn't need to leave the cosy zone just for the sake of it. If you're growing and feeling appreciated, it makes sense to expand it further instead of quitting. You have a choice to enrich it, add value, and grow within the existing environment. The other side of the coin is when you assess alternatives and are willing to work hard to master new skills. You create the space to uplift yourself in the process. If you can afford some time, money, and energy, it makes sense to explore newer terrains, gain new perspectives, and expand the existing horizon. It is alright even if you do not start with any passion. The thing about passion is that it can help you, but also hurt you if you are too rigid and vain about it.

Even if you're not certain what you're passionate about, you can still succeed without it. Think of it this way. Not being able to identify a passion can help you explore further and be more realistic. You may even feel liberated by your lack of it and develop the wisdom on what you like in life, and, most importantly, what you don't! You open yourself to transformation by opening your mental locks. The key to opening any lock is to be mindful of your decisions and choose your battles wisely. What may work for others may not work for you and vice versa. Life has multiple shades than simple black and white. You need to figure out if you are walking towards something you should be avoiding, or running away from something you should be facing. Evaluating the essential aspects, and the ones that need to be avoided, contributes to a more fulfilling journey in the right direction. How you see and value yourself depends on your mental conditioning. It is prudent to take two steps backwards to reflect and then leap forward. Your brain reciprocates positively when you focus on working hard and channelise your emotions into having quality and dedicated time for your peace of mind. It backfires when you're dragging yourself. The risks of burnout, physical ailments, and disturbances in mental makeup do not help in any way. The rewards of life are more impressive and sustainable when you are genuinely curious, enthusiastic, and upgrading yourself for the love of learning and development and not for impressing others. When you focus on self-development and are content from within, you shine. You develop a greater capacity to be in a stronger position to influence those around you in the role of a coach or a mentor.

What matters is whether you feel happy about what you are doing or not. I came across this powerful story on the web that seems quite relevant here.

There was a young entrepreneur.

> *Her chocolate chip cookies were a hit. She loved baking them, and her passion reflected on her face as she baked them. As the business grew, she got busy. She expanded the product line and included many fancy desserts, including intricate pastries and exotic-flavoured ice creams. The products did well, and she started earning more than ever.*
>
> *One day, a child walked into her store and asked, "Do you have any chocolate chip cookies?"*
>
> *She paused and had to say 'No'.*
>
> *The child refused to buy anything else and left.*
>
> *She sat down for some time.*
>
> *The realisation that she hadn't baked her favourite signature cookies in years hit hard. She stood up, put on her apron, collected the ingredients, and got ready to bake a batch of cookies. With the first bite, memories of her early baking days flooded her mind and gave her an unparalleled joy she hadn't experienced in years.*
>
> *In the hustle and bustle of life,*
>
> *In the name of progress or work commitments, you may sometimes miss the things that you loved doing the most. Retain the zeal and a beginner's mindset. Be like a gardener who plants with care and then steps back to allow the sun, rain, and soil to take over, intervening only when necessary. This will create a more natural-looking and healthier garden where plants can adapt and thrive in the existing environment.*

On a lighter note, you should also know when to remain quiet. An amusing incident from my hostel days perfectly illustrates this principle.

On a holiday morning, my friend and I decided to wake up early to enjoy hot, fluffy Indian fried ample bread (Puris) from our hostel mess without the usual long queue. The puris were irresistible, and we eagerly filled our plates with them and chickpea curry (Chole). Delighted by our early bird success, we even complimented the mess boy on the delicious, piping-hot meal. There was a slight tanginess in the curry, and we loved that creative twist. Perhaps, so we presumed, it was a touch of curd for extra flavour! We ate till we belched and then returned to our room to lay flat on our cosy beds. Little did we know, we were about to star in our self-inflicted comedy of errors. Approximately half an hour later, the peaceful morning was interrupted by a commotion in the mess hall. We heard some ramblings and peeped out of our window. The hostel warden had arrived, and whispers of stale chickpea curry filled the air. It turned out that the chickpea curry we had so heartily enjoyed and praised was musty and spoiled. Complaints had reached the warden, and a mini-crisis was unfolding right before our eyes. My friend and I exchanged confused and sheepish glances. To think we had eaten so much and had even complimented the mess boy for the 'delicious' meal!

Looking back, this amusing episode highlights the importance of addressing minor irritants before they become major problems. Our assumption that the food would be fresh in the morning led us to overlook the critical detail of its actual condition—a seemingly minor issue that could have had significant consequences. Thankfully, we survived the ordeal unscathed and managed to digest the questionable meal without incident. To date, it makes me wonder if it was luck or the intestinal fortitude of young age. What mattered then, however, was that we were able to read the room and keep our revolutionary love for that morning's meal a secret that is finally being revealed here today.

Disclaimer: I am not advocating silence when one must own up to mistakes. There is beauty in being honest, and it requires courage to face the consequences too. There are times when taking responsibility is crucial, but this incident taught me that sometimes, silence is the better path, especially when speaking up doesn't improve the situation. Leadership involves the wisdom to discern when words are necessary and when it's more appropriate to let things pass gracefully.

Choosing your battles wisely means cutting the noise to focus on what truly matters in life. Conflicts, politics, arguments, and strained relationships at home or office drain your energy. You may have found yourself more exhausted in handling emotions than doing your office work. Engaging in everything every time is counterproductive. It is essential to preserve your energy for prioritising significant issues in life. When you govern your reactions and actions, it can be a game-changer. Not all issues may be aligned with your values or goals. Their importance could be bifurcated under the categories of temporary inconvenience or of future significance. Not everything will warrant confrontation or involvement. The tenacity of your emotions will determine how you lead yourself. In handling the balance between controlling and letting go, potential unfolds, and greatness blooms.

In a world filled with challenges and choices to make each day, it's important to understand when to take action and when to pause for thought. Be it contemplating whether to dive into a discussion or weighing career paths, not every decision demands an instant answer. It's essential to assess whether the matter holds significance in relation to your goals and aspirations, or if it merely serves as a diversion. If a dilemma doesn't resonate with your overarching objectives, it's perfectly acceptable to release it from your focus instead of getting distracted by details. Remind yourself that sometimes the wisest choice is to refrain from getting entangled in some situations. Do you wonder how much time people have when they keep arguing with others on social media? Similarly, not every disagreement or argument (with anyone, be it friends, peers, bosses, parents, in-laws, siblings) needs to be prolonged. Step away for some time, if needed, or divert the topic. It's okay to even keep quiet at times and just listen, or come back to it later with more logical angles to gain fresh perspective. When all else fails, seek help.

The WISE framework given below can be used to help you evaluate the *noise* and make informed decisions about whether to engage in it or let it go. Your emotional mastery will act as a crucial agent in following these steps when faced with a dilemma or for decision-making.

Steps	Questions	Action
Weigh the importance (W),	Is this distraction significant enough for me to engage in it?	Determine the importance of the distraction. Identify if it aligns with long-term goals.
Identify Consequences (I)	Which potential outcomes can emerge from this (emotion/distraction)?	Weigh up the pros and cons of addressing or ignoring the distraction.
Scrutinise emotions (S).	What emotions am I experiencing, and how can they affect my judgement?	Investigate the root cause of the distraction, its origin, and relevance.
Evaluate the stakes (E),	What are the stakes involved?	Assess the stakes as High or Low, Trivial or Significant, and decide if it's worth addressing.

Here is an example of how to use this framework to handle a situation.

Imagine a workplace scenario where a colleague or a supervisor repeatedly takes credit for your ideas. Instead of immediately confronting them, you can choose to evaluate the situation:

- ***Weigh the Importance:*** Is this a one-time occurrence, or a pattern that could affect your career advancement? Ask yourself if the issue at hand is significant enough to warrant a confrontation. Does it align with your core values or long-term goals? Will it matter in the future, or is it a temporary inconvenience?
- ***Identify Consequences:*** Will confronting that person lead to a resolution, or could it create a hostile work environment? Assess the potential outcomes of engaging in the battle. What are the possible benefits and drawbacks? How will it affect your relationships, reputation, and well-being?
- ***Scrutinise Emotions:*** Are you feeling slighted because of ego, or is there a genuine concern about fairness and recognition? Emotions can cloud judgement. Take a moment to step back and evaluate your feelings. Are you reacting out of anger, frustration, or ego? Aim to approach the situation with a clear, rational mindset.
- ***Evaluate the Stakes:*** Is this affecting your job satisfaction and performance, or is it something you can address through other channels? Weigh the stakes involved. Is the issue trivial or significant? Will resolving it bring about a positive change, or is it a minor inconvenience that can be overlooked?

Seeking alternatives to immediate reactions is possible in such situations that may test your patience on some days. Can you document your contributions more clearly, or constructively discuss the issue? Sometimes, battles can be avoided through compromise, negotiation, or simply by choosing to let go. You may also want to look for alternative ways to address the issue without escalating conflict. By considering these factors, you might decide that a calm, private conversation, or seeking advice from a mentor, could be more effective than sulking or going for a public confrontation.

Another tool that can be used here is *Force Field Analysis*, developed by Kurt Lewin, a German-American social psychologist and organisational development pioneer, in the 1940s. It is a powerful decision-making tool that can help you identify and analyse the forces driving or restricting a proposed change. By identifying and assessing these forces, you can better understand the dynamics at play. You can then develop strategies to fortify driving forces or reduce restraining ones, ultimately guiding you towards a more informed and strategic decision.

Use the following template to analyse the driving and restraining forces affecting your decision or change. Fill in the table below to list and evaluate the forces.

Issue/ Change in life or organisation	**Driving Forces**	**Force Strength**	**Restraining Forces**	**Force Strength**

1) Mention the decision you need to take (change, action).
2) List the Driving Forces and Restraining Forces related to your decision or change.
3) Evaluate the strength of each force (e.g., Low, Medium, High).
4) Analyse the forces to determine the feasibility of moving forward with the decision or change.

Some examples are given below. More details can be added under each section.

Issue/ Change	Driving Forces	Force Strength	Restraining Forces	Force Strength
Replacing machines	Increased Efficiency	High	High Implementation Costs	High
Whether to relocate for a new job,	Career Advancement with a high salary and new	High	Family Disruption (spouse's job, children's education).	High
Managing a Conflict with a Spouse about Spending Habits	Desire for Financial Stability.	High for one partner Medium for another	Emotional Sensitivity (heated arguments)	High

Analysis: You can see the total number of driving forces versus the restraining forces and address accordingly. In the above-mentioned examples, only one sub-force has been mentioned against each issue. The numbers can be much higher.

Decision: To move forward, it would be vital to develop strategies to diminish the restraining forces. If these issues can be addressed effectively, the benefits of the change would likely outweigh the drawbacks.

Figure 3 in chapter 2 of this book, *Path to Action flowchart,* can also be used here for more precision in decision making. Clarity in strategic decision-making requires a clear understanding of your values, goals, and the impact of each conflict on your life. By evaluating the importance, consequences, emotions, stakes, and alternatives, you can navigate the path ahead more effectively, preserving your energy for the battles that truly matter. Next time you find yourself on the brink of a conflict or dilemma, pause and ask yourself: is this worth my energy? This approach not only leads to more successful outcomes but also contributes to a more harmonious and fulfilling life.

It is important to integrate data into your decision-making process to provide a factual basis for evaluating the driving and restraining forces. However, understanding the story behind the data is equally crucial. A deeper understanding of what led to a data point reveals the context, underlying drives, and potential inferences that numbers alone cannot capture. This distinctive insight allows you to make more primed and nuanced decisions, ensuring that both the data and the human factors are considered.

Broaden your mental horizon to gain clarity and depth, unburdened by noise and empowered by insight. The more clutter-free you become, the lighter your wings will be to fly and soar higher.

- How often do I find myself stuck in old patterns of thinking?
- What can I do to ensure that I am always open and receptive to new possibilities and perspectives?
- Can I admit to being wrong when I am?
- What are the potential outcomes of my decision?
- What emotions cloud my judgment?
- What are the sources of my trigger?
- How can I be more rational in approaching an unpleasant person or situation?
- When I say 'Yes' to something, what am I saying 'No' to?
- What am I saying 'No' to when I say 'Yes' to something?

Conclusion

The Inner Summit: Mastering Leadership from Within

(Image generated by DALL·E for Leadoscope)

Developing the right temperament is an everyday endeavour

I firmly believe that any journey of leading self begins with the right questions. After all, leadership is about leading yourself first before others. In a world saturated with external noise and relentless demands, the most consistent guidance must emerge from within—your values, convictions, and sense of purpose. Many struggle to connect with these powerful internal forces. The reality is not ideal. All is well till that one mistake and oversight, or that one unseen and incomprehensible knock that life throws at you, and you are caught off-guard. The tectonic plates can shift overnight, shaking and shattering the ground beneath! The biggest impediment is to think you are the strongest and the mightiest; inevitable to the family, office, society, and the world; perhaps even God's gift to mankind!

When the Titanic sank on a fateful night in April 1912, it shook and shocked the world. It was a tragedy of immense proportions. A question that bothered everyone was: how could it sink? Hadn't the experts claimed this ship was unsinkable?

No matter how well-prepared individuals or organisations are with their supposedly foolproof strategies, external factors, unexpected occurrences, and crises can put everything to the test. History is testimony to some of the largest empires, like the Greeks, the Ottomans, and the Mongols, falling like a pack of cards. We have a modern-day equivalence in the fall of mighty organisations like Lehman Brothers, a global financial services firm, that filed for bankruptcy in 2008. To think it used to be one of the top dream companies to work for! An over-reliance on risky mortgage-backed securities, coupled with some bad decisions, led to its downfall. Similarly, former mobile phone industry stalwarts such as Nokia or Blackberry (Research in Motion) failed to innovate and delayed in adapting to the smartphone revolution, leading to losing their ground to the competitors. There was a significant decline in their sales, and they lost the battle.

Kingfisher Airlines in India, founded by Vijay Mallya, and once a mark of luxury and class in Indian aviation, had to wind up its operations in 2012 due to heavy debt and losses. The case for some of the top companies like Essar Steel, Bhushan Steel, Reliance Communications, and Jet Airways, amongst many others, are no different. Fleeting success saw several startups, like Byju's, or celebrities soar to the top like shooting stars on a growth trajectory and reign like kings, only to burn out and fade into insolvency just as quickly even before the ink dried on their headlines.

The COVID-19 outbreak that shook the world and disrupted plans across every conceivable sector, showcased the critical importance of adaptability and resilience in the face of unforeseen challenges. Despite meticulous preparations and strategic forecasts that businesses, governments, and individuals had in place, the swift and unprecedented nature of the outbreak forced a swift re-evaluation of nearly every aspect of operations and life. The ability to pivot quickly, innovate solutions on the fly, and implement new procedures to safeguard health and continue services became the cornerstones of survival and success. The outbreak of the COVID-19 pandemic also highlighted the need for robust contingency planning and strong leadership at every level to be able to handle, not just minor adjustments to existing strategies, but also complete overhauls in extreme scenarios. This event proved that while strong strategies are indispensable, the flexibility to adapt, and the resilience to persevere are equally crucial.

Factoring in environmental uncertainties and thinking on your feet during a crisis is not a one-day learning. The ability to lead is not merely about influencing others; it's fundamentally about understanding and directing oneself. People with inner strength can be the forerunners in such situations. A robust inner compass is essential in effectively leading both yourself and others. This internal guide serves as the foundation of authentic leadership, providing a stable and consistent framework from which your decisions and actions emanate, fostering trust and inspiring those around you. It acts like a guiding light that aligns your actions with the deep values that you develop by focusing on your mindset and skills, along with long-term goals. Your decision-making turns robust because you no longer get swayed by fleeting circumstances or emotions. You lead yourself with a deep understanding of what you embody and stand for. This self-awareness is critical to staying focused, managing emotions, and being resilient vis-a-vis the intricacy of life. You can lead others by example of your consistency, integrity, and reliability. Building trust and credibility through clarity and decisiveness are cornerstones of effective leadership. Your actions build your ethical grounding that also influences the organisational culture positively.

The goal is to build and sustain a more cohesive and purpose-driven environment for everyone involved. It is imperative for you to lead by example for people to follow suit.

Ultimately, leadership is not a place but an unfolding path of self-discovery and development. It all starts with the silent courage to lead oneself – to face the imposter within, dance with the stillness of boredom, and find clarity amidst the noise. And while we extend our influence on others, let's never forget that true leadership is a matter of empathy, collaboration, and the stories we tell and live. Just as nature flourishes within diversity and balance, so we can try to nurture these qualities in ourselves and our communities. Beyond the world of success and failure is the essence of leadership: to connect, to inspire, and to make a world where every voice matters.

In this context, I would like to share a well-known parable with my students every year and cannot resist penning it down here for you.

A man dreamt of teaching his pet frog to fly, convinced that with enough determination, anything was possible. Despite the frog's logical protests—frogs aren't meant to fly—the man persisted. Each day, the frog had to try jumping out of progressively higher windows in a desperate bid to learn to fly. It failed every time. All the aspects - management and motivational theories, discussion on the bigger picture, and feedback sessions after each day of action - were in place. Yet the frog couldn't fly despite his best efforts. Tragically, the story ends with the frog's inevitable demise, having never achieved the impossible task set before him.

The man concluded that the frog was not smart enough, and next time, he'd get a smarter frog.

What stands out about this parable is that the man failed to recognise that his frog could speak, a remarkable and unique skill. Instead of leveraging this extraordinary competency, he focused solely on an impossible goal of making the frog learn how to fly, which would help him make money. It also shows that he did not pay heed to the frog's pleas (feedback).

I am sure you can recall at least some people, be it a boss, friend, acquaintance, or even a family member, who consider themselves to be no less than God. No matter how much others try to challenge, correct, or prove them wrong, they simply don't listen. They choose to ignore the truth and brush issues under the carpet, refusing to address the elephant in the room. An air of infallibility surrounds their head like an imaginary halo. In sharp contrast are those who focus on identifying and recognising uniqueness (theirs or others'). They are gifted. It pays to appreciate extraordinary competencies and not let those get lost in pursuit of other goals.

Ambitious goals are important, but they must also be grounded. You must aim high, yet remember that your style may not work in every situation with everyone. You need to be observant and flexible. The same is true for life. You may often find yourself on a hedonic treadmill, constantly after the next source of happiness or success. The dissatisfaction comes when you discover that the satisfaction is fleeting. This relentless chase can place your unique talents and qualities on the back burner. In your comparison mode too, you may focus on your voids instead of gifts. The little things with the potential for true fulfilment and purpose often go underutilised as you focus on external achievements and validations. Know when to pivot. Persistence is valuable, but not when it leads to repeated failure. Flexibility in approach is the key. Great leadership involves balancing ambition with practicality, and pushing boundaries while respecting the inherent capabilities of the team. Adapting strategies based on realistic assessments can do wonders.

What's your perspective?

I sincerely hope this book has offered you a glimmer of insight, a moment of reflection, or a tool to help you navigate your unique leadership journey, whether in leading self or others. My objective was to share take you on a path to approach life with some alternate perspectives. If the book has resonated with you, sparked a new perception, or helped you take even one step forward, I am grateful to have been a small part of your growth and development.

While I have done my best to share some of my insights with you, I recognise that unintentional mistakes may have been made along the way. If so, I ask for your understanding and hope that the overall message still serves you well. Please feel free to point out those mistakes, if any, by writing an email to me. I will rectify them in the next edition. In the end, the true measure of this book's success lies not in its pages, but in the positive impact it may have on your life and the lives that you impact.

The movie Ratatouille summed it up the best: *anyone can cook.* It seems similar when it comes to leadership—anyone can take the role without needing titles, loads of experience, or special privileges to do so effectively and meaningfully. Leadership isn't for those with positions or fancy degrees hanging on their walls—it is about stepping up to the plate and inspiring others in their own unique style. Anyone has the potential to be a leader by deciding to do so.

Anyone can lead.

Leadership is about creating a ripple effect. As you take steps to lead yourself and others, may you find the strength to be the perennial learner, ever-evolving, ever-growing, and ever-inspiring. May people love, admire and respect you not for your position but for your disposition.

End Notes

Chapter 1 Beyond Myopia: Power and Balance

Gallwey, T. (2000). The Inner Game of Work: Focus, Learning, Pleasure and Mobility in the Workplace. Random House.

Wheel of Life: *Meyer, P. J. (1960). The Wheel of Life, Success Motivation Institute.*

Chapter 2 The Elemental Forces of Development: Emotions and Letting Go

The Art of Letting Go, by Nick Trenton

Trenton, N. (2023). The Art of Letting Go: Stop Overthinking, Stop Negative Spirals and Find Emotional Freedom. Pimiento Books.

The Wheel of Emotions

Plutchik, R. (1980). A general psychoevolutionary theory of emotion. In R. Plutchik & H. Kellerman (eds.), Emotion: Theory, research, and experience, Theories of emotion (Vol. 1, pp. 3–33). New York: Academic Press.

Dopamine Nation: Finding Balance in the Age of Indulgence

Lembke, A. (2021). Dopamine Nation: Finding Balance in the Age of Indulgence. Dutton, USA.

Chapter 3 Managing Mosquito-ism

Pomodoro Technique

https://www.forbes.com/sites/bryancollinseurope/2020/03/03/the-pomodoro-technique/

Eisenhower Matrix

https://asana.com/resources/eisenhower-matrix

Chapter 4 Personal Branding and Pragmatic Humility

Faisal Khan - khanglobalstudies.com, www.youtube.com/@khangsresearchcentre168

Revant Himatsingka - @Foodpharmer (Instagram and YouTube)

Sindhutai Sapkal: https://www.sindhutaisapkal.org/team/dr-sindhutai-sapkal

Chhavi Rajawat- @chhavi.rajawat (Instagram)

Phoolbasanbai- @phoolbasanbai (Instagram)

Chapter 5 Channeling Imposter Syndrome

Six Thinking Hats by Edward de Bono, https://www.debonogroup.com/services/core-programs/six-thinking-hats/.

Chapter 6 Communication and Influence

Freytag's Pyramid for Storytelling: *Freytag, G. (1895). Freytag's Technique of the Drama: An Exposition of Dramatic Composition and Art (E. J. MacEwan, Trans.). S.C. Griggs.*

Chapter 7 Beyond Boredom: Embracing Possibilities

The Einstellung Effect: *Luchins, A. S. (1942). Mechanization in problem solving: The effect of Einstellung, Psychological monographs, 54 (6), i.*

Bounded Rationality: *Simon, H. (1957). A Behavioral Model of Rational Choice. Models of Man. Social and Rational: Mathematical Essays on Rational Human Behavior in a Social Setting/Wiley.*

Crucibles of Leadership: *Bennis, W. G., & Thomas, R. J. (2002). Crucibles of Leadership. Harvard Business Review, 80.*

Chapter 8 Navigating Relationships

Johari Window: *Luft, J., & Ingham, H. (1955). The Johari window, a graphic model of interpersonal awareness. Proceedings of the western training laboratory in group development, 246.*

Chapter 9 Mindset Mastery: Beyond Success and Failure

The Concept of Black Swan: *Taleb, N. N. (2007). The Black Swan: The Impact of the Highly Improbable, Random House.*

Chapter 10 Dilemma and Decision Making: Filtering the Noise

Emotional Intelligence: *Goleman, D. (1995). Emotional Intelligence: Why It Can Matter More Than IQ, Bantam Books.*

Cognitive Dissonance: *Festinger, L. (1957). A Theory of Cognitive Dissonance, Stanford University Press.*

The Hidden Brain by Shankar Vedantam: *Vedantam, S. (2010). The Hidden Brain: How Our Unconscious Minds Elect Presidents, Control Markets, Wage Wars, and Save Our Lives, Random House.*

Meet the Author

Sonal Shree (PhD, MBA) is an acclaimed academic with extensive experience shaping some of the brightest young minds in the country. She is currently an Associate Professor at Symbiosis Institute of Business Management, Pune, a constituent of Symbiosis International University, Pune, India. Her facilitation has earned numerous accolades for its depth and practical relevance. Beyond academia, she is a Leadership Development and Impactful Communication Trainer and Consultant, a certified Executive Coach, a blogger with the Times of India (TOI blogs), and a Public Speaker. Known for her ability to distill complex ideas into actionable insights, she has mentored countless people, especially mid-career professionals, embrace their unique strengths and lead with authenticity and confidence.

Leadoscope is her way of reaching out to a broader audience seeking to achieve personal growth and professional excellence. Through practical tools and insights, she hopes to remind the readers that a leadership mindset starts with self-belief, even in doubt, and thrives by embracing challenges with confidence, growth, support, and solutions.

(Scan to connect with the author)

www.ingramcontent.com/pod-product-compliance
Lightning Source LLC
LaVergne TN
LVHW042354150826
845671LV00002B/117

* 9 7 9 8 8 9 5 8 8 2 5 1 1 *